Globalisation and Second Language Identity

Manfred Man-fat Wu

Globalisation and Second Language Identity

Opportunities, Challenges, and the Importance of Morality

Manfred Man-fat Wu
School of Open Learning
Hong Kong Metropolitan University
Kowloon, Hong Kong

ISBN 978-3-031-68247-6   ISBN 978-3-031-68248-3   (eBook)
https://doi.org/10.1007/978-3-031-68248-3

Cover illustration: © Melisa Hasan

This Palgrave Macmillan imprint is published by the registered company Springer Nature Switzerland AG
The registered company address is: Gewerbestrasse 11, 6330 Cham, Switzerland

If disposing of this product, please recycle the paper.

This book is dedicated to my wife, Anne Chun Miao, who has always been supportive and loving throughout the years.

CONTENTS

PART I

Introduction

CHAPTER 1

Introduction

Abstract This chapter sets the stage for subsequent discussions and provides the background for this book. Globalisation has radically transformed many aspects of contemporary individuals. However, compared to other aspects, relatively meagre attention has been given to how globalisation influences second language (L2) identity. This book aims to draw attention to this relatively neglected area, arguing that L2 identity is a key construct not only in the acquisition of an L2 but many other aspects of individuals' well-being. Individuals' learning experiences contribute to the construction of their L2 identity, and their L2 identity constructed over the years in turn influences their perceptions of L2 learning. This book discusses how globalisation influences L2 identity, as well as the opportunities and challenges globalisation has brought for the construction and maintenance of L2 identity. One major conclusion of this book is that the increasing extent of cultural exchange due to globalisation results in dilemmas of self, especially in terms of morality. This is because language and values are intimately related, and there are conflicting demands in terms of the morality of different cultures. Therefore, morality, a dimension that has almost been completely neglected, is proposed to be included as a key component in fostering L2 identity. As autonomy is an integral part of identity and a contributor to successful L2 learning, how to reconceptualise and foster L2 autonomy in the age of globalisation is selected to be another topic discussed in this book. Finally, globalisation has posed new demands for L2 teachers and teachers need

M. M. Wu, *Globalisation and Second Language Identity*, https://doi.org/10.1007/978-3-031-68248-3_1

to transform their identity in order to remain effective in their profession. This book proposes the essential qualities that constitute L2 teacher identity in the context of globalisation.

Keywords Globalisation · L2 identity · Morality · L2 autonomy · L2 teacher identity

INTRODUCTION

Globalisation, "the processes by virtue of which the sovereign nation states intermingle and interweave through transnational actors" (Roldán 2018: 110), exerts profound and widespread influences on different aspects of modern life, even though it is often argued that the majority of people still live a local life (Giddens 2006). In fact, globalisation has radically transformed many aspects of contemporary individuals, from consumption patterns, entertainment, travel, career, personal finance, and family, as well as social and political lives. Second language (L2) identity is no exception and deserves special attention, given the role of English as a lingua franca, which implies that the English language and its acquisition influence the identity of a substantial proportion of the global population. Despite its significance, compared to other aspects such as multilingualism (Gao and Zheng 2019), global citizenship (Torres and Bosio 2020), and internationalisation of higher education (Doiz et al. 2013; Kamyab and Raby 2023), how globalisation influences L2 identity has seldom been discussed.

The increasing extent of globalisation has substantially expanded individuals' frequency of contact with individuals from other parts of the world (Jensen 2021). Some examples are the use of social media for entertainment and consumption, job and business purposes (such as conducting online meetings and virtual business events, as well as travelling both for tourism and business purposes). The use of a lingua franca is inevitable as more frequent contact with sojourners of various parts of the globe means more frequent use of a common language.

This book aims to draw attention to this relatively neglected area and argues that L2 identity is a key construct not only in the acquisition of an L2 but in many other aspects of individuals' well-being. This is because the unchallenged status as a lingua franca has resulted in English learning mandatory for many students across the globe. English learning is included in the national curriculum of many countries, for example, Korea (National Curriculum Information Center n.d.) and Japan (MEXT 2011), with the aim of enabling citizens to stay economically competitive and be able to participate in cross-national and international affairs effectively.

Learning experiences contribute to the construction of L2 identity, which is "any aspect of a person's identity that is related to their knowledge and use of a second language" (Benson et al. 2013: 17), and L2 identity constructed over the years in turn influences learners' perceptions on English learning. The attitudes of the community towards English also contribute to the stance of policymakers, employers, parents, and other stakeholders involved in L2 education, and they exert direct and indirect influences on the L2 identity of learners. In addition to being influenced by outside forces, L2 identity at the same time influences individuals' subjectivities and behaviours related to their L2 learning, for example, learning motivation (Dörnyei et al. 2006), the amount of time and effort they invest in learning (Sung 2020), frequency of using English, and their use of English situations in which they have a choice of using English (Block and Cameron 2002). L2 identity also has long-term influences on individuals' academic achievement and career development (Rutgers et al. 2024).

This book explores issues related to globalisation and L2 identity. It discusses how globalisation influences L2 identity, and the opportunities and challenges globalisation has brought for the construction and maintenance of L2 identity. One major conclusion of this book is that the increasing extent of cultural exchange due to globalisation results in dilemmas of self, especially in terms of morality. This is because language and values are intimately related, that language is a means for expressing moral values, making moral judgements, discussing moral issues, and most importantly, shaping and teaching moral values. In the context of globalisation, there are conflicting moral demands from different cultures. Therefore, morality, a relatively neglected dimension, is proposed to be included as a key component in fostering L2 identity. As autonomy is an integral part of identity and a contributor to successful L2 learning, how to foster autonomy in the age of globalisation is also discussed in this book.

As members of the globalised community, L2 teachers are themselves not only influenced by globalisation per se but also have the obligation to foster positive L2 identity among their students. According to Sun (2020), successful global citizenship education (GCE) requires learners to possess an identity and attachment to the global community. In applying UNESCO's (2015) framework of global citizenship education, Sun (2020) recommends the notion of global citizenship be treated as an identity, a sense of belonging to the global community. Therefore, a chapter of this book is devoted to the essential qualities L2 teachers need for effective L2 teaching, especially in relation to L2 identity, in the globalised context. The final part of this book concludes the discussions made in the book and makes recommendations on theory, pedagogy, and research.

In the remainder of this chapter, the major themes, namely, morality, globalisation, and L2 identity, which form the conceptual framework for the entire book, will be introduced. The links between these themes will also be pointed out.

Morality

In simple terms, morality is concerned with the principles of right and wrong (Oxford University Press 2024). The Encyclopedia Britannica (Britannica 2023) provides a more detailed definition of morality, referring to it as "the moral beliefs and practices of a culture, community, or religion or a code or system of moral rules, principles, or values". According to Curry et al. (2019), morality functions to promote cooperation through emphasising mutual respect, care for one another, and equality. De Villiers (2023) extends the conceptualisation of Curry et al. (2019) and distinguishes between the biological and the cultural/religious origins of morality. The former shares Curry et al.'s (2019) view, that there is a need for cooperation among human individuals for biological survival. The latter view is related to the capacity of human individuals to use language, that is through language human beings can be motivated to act in ways suggested by the moral rules approved by community.

The following definition of morality offered by De Villiers (2023) is highly accessible across diverse academic and research disciplines:

> '[m]orality is a normative social institution with distinctive and stable core constituents: a core function of enhancing cooperation in communities by providing normative guidance to members on the fair advancement of wellbeing, a set of moral values attuned to the fulfilment of this function, a

set of mechanisms to motivate people to act in accordance with the moral values and approved ways to make moral decisions in concrete situations based on the moral values. At the same time, morality is a flexible social institution that adapts to changes in the social and cultural environment (1).

Given the long history and the broad coverage of the notion of morality, it is necessary to specify the conceptualisation adopted in this book. In this book, Kant's moral theory will be adopted, given Kant's (e.g., 2007) due consideration on globalisation and morality, as represented by his emphasis on human rights in the context of cosmopolitanism (Wu 2020). This book argues that fulfilling duties to others through taking action as proposed by Hegel (1977), a post-Kantian philosopher belonging to the philosophical movement of German Idealism as Kant, is equally if not more important than duties themselves. In this book, morality refers to awareness of one's duties to others and its fulfilment through taking action. Action taking is of particular relevance to globalisation because it has created new opportunities for citizens to engage in local and international affairs, for example, by offering material and intangible support to anti-war movements (Gaventa and Tandon 2010). At the same time, action taking resonates well with UNESCO's (2015) conceptualisation of global citizenship, which has been widely adopted in many countries (see Akkari and Maleq 2020).

The basic tenet of German Idealism is that human cognition determines the appearances of objects as opposed to the view that things in themselves have their own appearance. Regarding morality, Kant (2002) emphasises duty and obligation. Hegel attacked Kant's moral theory as a kind of formalism devoid of practical application in real life and proposed his idea of acting out pure duties (e.g., Hegel 1977).

GLOBALISATION AND GLOBAL CITIZENSHIP AS HUMAN RIGHTS

Kant is the founding father of the modern idea of globalisation and global citizenship as human rights (Wu 2020). Kant's seminal works *Perpetual peace* (1957) and *Idea for a universal history with a cosmopolitan aim* (2007) contain his main ideas on cosmopolitanism, which can be traced back to ancient Greece.

In his *Idea of a universal history on a cosmopolitical plan* (Kant 2007), Kant pointed out a need for international relations adjusted to laws between states. The development of a perfect state or civil society, including its internal and external relations, can be regarded as the realisation of a plan of nature (Kant 2007: 47). According to Kleingeld (1998, 2012), Kant's cosmopolitan law focuses on interactions between individuals and those of the states of which they are not citizens. One implication from the above account of Kant is that language serves a role in the protection of human rights in the public sphere.

Kant did not define cosmopolitanism and global citizenship explicitly, but in his seminal work on this topic, *Perpetual peace*, he pointed out the need for a "law of world citizenship". In the section of the "Third Definitive Article for a perpetual peace" of this book, Kant (1957) stated that "no one had more right than another to a particular part of the earth" (21) and "the human race can gradually be brought closer and closer to a constitution establishing world citizenship" (21). Kant paid particular attention to global citizenship, by which he refers to the rights and civil responsibilities that transcend national and geographic boundaries.

In Kant's philosophy, global citizenship is based on the premise that all rational individuals are members of a single community with shared morality. The above conceptualisation reflects that the idea of global citizenship is related to Kant's morality as discussed in his *Critique of pure reason* (Kant 1978), *Critique of practical reason* (Kant 1978), and related works such as *Groundwork of the metaphysics of morals* (Kant 2002). Kant uses his transcendental deduction described in his *Critique of pure reason* to derive his "Categories", which are cognitive schemas common to all individuals. These "Categories" provide the foundation for guidelines on moral actions, which Kant constructed as "Categorical Imperatives". In his *Groundwork of the metaphysics of morals*, Kant (2002) proposes the concept of individual right that "every action which by itself or by its maxim enables the freedom of each individual's will to co-exist with the freedom of everyone else in accordance with a universal law" (Kant 2002: 133). Kant regards morality as based on reasoning, a core notion of the Enlightenment. Thus, global citizenship and cosmopolitanism, which is moral in nature, form parts of Kant's entire philosophical system.

In *Perpetual peace*, Kant emphasises the equal rights among states in diverse aspects. One implication is that no one language should dominate other languages, the stance this book adopts. In describing how cosmopolitanism should be structured, particularly in the section "The law of nations shall be founded on a federation of free states" (Kant 1957: 18), Kant contends that a supranational body, a league that moves beyond bilateral and multilateral relations between state, is required. *Perpetual peace* begins with six "Preliminary Articles" which laid down the fundamental principles for the maintenance of peace between nations. The three strict principles proposed in this part are that there should be no provision reserved for future war, no interference in government between states, and no acts of hostility to the opposing state during war. The remaining three are broader in scope. They describe the core themes of Kant's moral philosophy, that there should be no dominance of one state over another by inheritance, exchange, purchase, or donation, no standing armies, and no arrangement of debts with a friction state. In the second part of the book, there are three "Definitive Articles" which describe how cosmopolitanism should be structured. It is in this part that Kant gave a direct account of cosmopolitanism and global citizenship as described.

Two representatives in the recent discussions on Kant's cosmopolitanism are Appiah (2006) and Kleingeld (1998, 2012). Appiah (2006) extends Kant's conceptualisation that an individual's obligation to a foreign other should go beyond his/her obligations towards his fellow members of his immediate community. Kleingeld (2012) made the first attempt at a full-scale philosophical study of Kant's cosmopolitanism with the aim of clarifying the misunderstandings of Kant's ideas. The first theme Kleingeld discusses is that cosmopolitanism is compatible with patriotism. The second theme is Kant's advocacy of the existence of a plurality of individual states. In her discussion, Kleingeld (2012) aims to clarify a common misunderstanding on the accusation of the inability to form one universal state as proposed in Kant's theory. According to her, the non-coercive league of nation is only a beginning step for the establishment of a cosmopolitan political order. The third theme that Kleingeld discusses is cosmopolitan right, or the right to hospitality. Kant's egalitarian form of cosmopolitanism allowed his theory to accommodate a wider range of cultural diversity. The last theme was economic justice and free trade. These two representatives highlight the role of obligation and rights in Kant's theory on global citizenship. Thus, Kant's idea of globalisation is heavily nuanced with human rights, duties, and morality.

Cavallar (2014) summarises the three camps in the historical development of hospitality right: the imperialist school, the society of states school, and cosmopolitan school. For the imperialist school, hospitality is an extensive natural right and could be enforced. Natural rights such as travel and trade, according to this school, are only means rather than ends to achieve the end of the spreading of the Gospel. The society of states school gradually gained importance in the eighteenth century after the popularity of the imperialist school. As its name suggests, the perspective adopted by this school is state-centred, which focuses on the right of the state to restrict trades. Hospitality is no longer treated as a natural right for this school. The third school regards hospitality as a natural right, but unlike the imperialist school, natural rights are treated as ends themselves rather than a means for achieving religious purposes. Kant's main difference with these three schools is that his focus on hospitality is trade and freedom to travel (i.e., interactions between individuals as described earlier) rather than the right to abode in a foreign country or to be a guest. However, Kant also argues that the right to present oneself to society is equally important in the concept of hospitality (Kant 1957; see also Cavallar 2014). Cavallar (2014) emphasises the importance of right in the realm of hospitality in Kant's theory.

One important implication of Kant's above philosophy is that globalisation which has accelerated and widened the interconnection and interdependence among individuals resulted in a need for transformation of morality, or in his terms the need to take into consideration cosmopolitan and hospitality rights. Kant has laid the backdrop for the discussions to be undertaken in this book, that globalisation gives rise to repercussions on the morality, which is part of the identity of L2 learners and teachers. In fact, it has been pointed out that globalisation impacts moral values (Jensen, 2021) and L2 teaching should assume moral responsibilities in the globalised era (see Sun and Buripakdi 2021). The moral elements of duties to others advocated by Kant and taking action to fulfil and realise moral duties by Hegel are proposed in this book as the means for overcoming the challenges for the identity of L2 learners and teachers.

The Role of Morality in L2 Identity

Identity is notoriously known to be a slippery term, as it refers to both commonalities and differences among individuals (Riley 2006). Identity is very often used to describe the characteristics that an individual shares with other members of a community and, at the same time those that distinguish him or her from others. In L2 research, identity is commonly conceptualised as a set of public and private beliefs related to L2 learning, which may differ in relational contexts. This is because in various relational contexts individuals interact with others of different social capacities and social expectations (e.g., Taylor et al. 2013). It is well established among L2 researchers that learning a new language is at the same time forming a new identity and language and identity are inseparable (e.g., Yuan and Mak 2018). Inherited from traditional disciplines such as sociolinguistics, psycholinguistics, and social constructivist which have been in currency in the last few decades, research on L2 identity has been characterised by a myriad of theoretical frameworks and focuses (see Wu 2023). Despite the diversified development in L2 identity theories, relatively puny attention has been given to the philosophical and moral aspects of L2 identity (Wu 2023). Rutgers et al. (2024) comment that research on L2 identity to date has been over-focusing on cognition. In fact, it has been well-documented that emotion such as empathy which constitutes morality is another core component of L2 identity, both for L2 learners and teachers (Mohammadi 2022; Rokita-Jaśkow and Werbińska 2023; Wang 2021).

Research on L2 identity has been dominated by the "essentialist" school.[1] One landmark in recent L2 identity research of this school is the large-scale longitudinal survey conducted by Dörnyei and his colleagues on L2 learning attitudes and motivation of Hungarian teenagers (Dörnyei and Csizér 2002; Dörnyei et al. 2006). Their findings confirm the pioneering notion of possible selves proposed by Markus and Nurius (1986),[2] and they developed their L2 Motivational Self System, with ideal self as the central concept and "ought-to-self", which is moral in nature, as the complementary concept. The main tenet of this theory is that the discrepancy between the current self and the future selves influenced by the ideal self and "ought-to-self" is a powerful motivator for individuals to learn an L2.

Mantero (2007) summarises the historical approaches to the study of L2 identity. They are the social-psychological, social-interactional, and

---

[1] The 'essentialist' school treats identity as a stable construct that can be measured and quantified, with the relationships between its components being analysed. See, for example, Dunmore (2021).

[2] Markus and Nurius (1986) introduce the concept of possible selves, which refers to what individuals might/would like/would not like to become, as a conceptual link between cognition and motivation.

post-structural. The social-psychological approach, according to him, is ethnolinguistic in nature and deals with issues such as cultural assimilation, acculturation, and ethnic relations. Its limited scope results in narrow application to the study of L2 identity. The social-psychological approaches that pay attention to social structural factors such as ethnicity also have limited applicability. The issues of power and multiple linguistic group membership pose difficulties for the ethnolinguistic approach, which is a branch of social-psychological approaches. The social-interactional approaches that centre on multilingualism and language choice on topics such as code-switching only have limited applicability to L2 identity research again because of their narrow focuses. Post-structural approaches focus on power relations, negotiation of meaning, individual subjectivity, fluidity of L2 identity, and the significant role of social context in influencing L2 identity. These themes make the post-structural theory better equipped for the study of L2 identity in the globalisation context. The post-structural approaches view identity as imposed, assumed, and negotiable (see Gao et al. 2015). What is important is that these approaches acknowledge the need for mutual recognition among individuals which enables the achievement of authentic and mediated relationships among individuals that sustain over time. Mutual recognition among nations is one of the prerequisites for the successful cultivation of a globalised L2 identity.[3] Mantero's (2007) summary indicates a trend that is highly related to the focus of this book, that is, the important roles played by morality.

All three approaches described above involve the judgement and evaluation of right and wrong, thus morality. Two examples are whether L2 learners should not use their native language to translate the target language they learn, and whose language standard should be adopted for assessing language proficiency. The social-psychological approaches deal with issues such as culture and ethnicity, which inevitably involve inequality, duties, and rights. The social-interactional approaches put particular stress on multilingualism, which again covers culture, value, and attitude. The post-structural approaches, according to Mantero (2007), explore issues such as power and subjectivity which are again intimately linked to a sense of right and wrong. This book concurs with the emphasis

---

[3] Browning (2011) provides a detailed account on the reasons for recognition among nations in the contemporary globalised world. Mutual recognition is also a core notion in Hegel's (1977) philosophy.

on power and subjectivity of the post-structuralist approaches. The above summary indicates that while there is a need for addressing the issue of a lack of consideration given to morality in the context of globalisation in L2 identity research, most historical and contemporary research approaches on this area are embedded with morality.

Second language acquisition (SLA) research, a branch of L2 research focusing on how an L2 is learned both in a natural setting or a formal classroom setting, has shifted its focus from the individual to the effects of social context on individuals over the past decades (Ricento 2005). In his review of the seminal theories on L2 identity in SLA research, Ricento (2005) comments that despite the attention given to social contexts, the historical theories did not put sufficient emphasis on "the interaction of an individual's multiple memberships based on gender, class, race, linguistic repertoire, or on how these memberships were understood and played out in different learning contexts" (898). Rutgers et al. (2024) share the same view, that in the contemporary multilingual and globalised context, multiple identity profiles have become common, and therefore, research on multiple memberships, especially those which take into accounts emotion and attitudes (elements that are intimately related to morality pointed out earlier) instead of mere cognition should be embarked upon. This book is partly a response to the call for taking into account the non-cognitive elements in the discussions L2 identity.

The importance of morality, or more specifically one's responsibilities to others and the community, has been well-documented, particularly from the perspective of possible selves (see Sahakyan et al. 2018). As suggested earlier, the "ought-to-self" component of this perspective, among the actual and ideal self, refers to the qualities an individual believes one ought to possess. For L2 learners, the "ought-to-self" prescribes the responsibilities learners regard as having to be fulfilled, for example, to study hard in learning the target language, respect cultural differences, appreciate diversity, and honesty in their L2 learning. For L2 teachers, examples of their moral obligations to learners are commitment to teaching, ethical teaching practices, and fairness.

Outline of This Book

This book discusses how globalisation influences L2 identity. In Chapter 2, the opportunities and challenges globalisation has brought for the construction and maintenance of L2 identity are introduced. The increasing extent of cultural exchange of globalisation results in dilemmas of self, especially in terms of morality. It is because language and values are intimately related, and there are conflicting demands on morality in different cultures. Therefore, morality is proposed to be included as a key component in fostering L2 identity. The dilemmas of self and the importance of morality are discussed in Chapters 3 and 4 respectively. As autonomy is an integral part of identity and a contributor to successful L2 learning, the need for reconceptualising L2 autonomy and ways to foster autonomy in the context of globalisation are discussed in Chapter 5. Globalisation has posed new demands for L2 teachers (Wu 2024) and teachers need to transform their identity in order to remain effective in their teaching. Chapter 6 proposes the essential qualities that constitute L2 teacher identity in the context of globalisation. Chapter 7 concludes this book by providing a summary of arguments undertaken in previous chapters and reiterates the role of morality in the research and nurturing of L2 identity for both L2 learners and teachers. This book ends with recommendations for future theoretical development, pedagogy, and research.

References

Akkari, Abdeljalil, and Katherine Maleq, eds. 2020. *Global citizenship education: Critical and international perspectives.* Cham: Springer. https://doi.org/10.1007/978-3-030-44617-8.

Appiah, Kwame Anthony. 2006. *Cosmopolitanism. Ethics in a world of strangers.* London: Penguin Books.

Benson, Phil, Barkhuizen, Gary, Bodycott, Peter, and Brown, Jill. 2013. Second language identity. In Phil Benson, Gary Barkhuizen, Peter Bodycott, and Jill Brown (Eds.), *Second language identity in narratives of study abroad*, 17–33. London: Palgrave Macmillan. https://doi.org/10.1057/9781137029423_2

Block, David, and Deborah Cameron. 2002. Introduction. In *Globalization and language teaching*, ed. David Block and Deborah Cameron, 1–10. London: Routledge.

Britannica, The Editors of Encyclopaedia. 29 Mar. 2024. Morality. In *Encyclopedia Britannica*. Retrieved 6 February 2024, from https://www.britannica.com/topic/morality

Browning, Gary. 2011. Hegel: Global theory and recognition. In *Global theory from Kant to Hardt and Negri*, ed. Gary Browning, 42–60. London: Palgrave Macmillan. https://doi.org/10.1057/9780230308541_3.

Cavallar, Georg. 2014. Kant and the right of world citizens: An historical interpretation. In *Critique of cosmopolitan reason: Timing and spacing the concept of world citizenship*, ed. Rebecka Lettevall and Kristian Petrov, 141–179. Bern: Peter Lang. https://doi.org/10.3726/978-3-0353-0620-0.

Curry, Oliver Scott, Daniel Austin Mullins, and Harvey Whitehouse. 2019. Is it good to cooperate? Testing the theory of morality-as-cooperation in 60 societies. *Current Anthropology* 60 (1): 47–69. https://doi.org/10.1086/701478.

De Villiers, D. Etienne. 2023. What is morality? A historical exploration. *Verbum Et Ecclesia* 44 (1): a2935. https://doi.org/10.4102/ve.v44i1.2935.

Doiz, Aintzane, David Lasagabaster, and Juan Sierra. 2013. Globalisation, internationalisation, multilingualism and linguistic strains in higher education. *Studies in Higher Education* 38 (9): 1407–1421. https://doi.org/10.1080/03075079.2011.642349.

Dörnyei, Zoltán, and Kata Csizér. 2002. Some dynamics of language attitudes and motivation: Results of a longitudinal nationwide survey. *Applied Linguistics* 23: 421–462. https://doi.org/10.1093/applin/23.4.421.

Dörnyei, Zoltán, Kata Csizér, and Nóra. Németh. 2006. *Motivation, language attitudes and globalization: A Hungarian perspective*. Clevedon: Multilingual Matters. https://doi.org/10.21832/9781853598876.

Dunmore, Stuart S. 2021. Emic and essentialist perspectives on Gaelic heritage: New speakers, language policy, and cultural identity in Nova Scotia and Scotland. *Language in Society* 50: 259–281. https://doi.org/10.1017/S0047404520000032.

Gao, Xuesong, and Yongyan Zheng. 2019. Multilingualism and higher education in Greater China. *Journal of Multilingual and Multicultural Development* 40 (7): 555–561. https://doi.org/10.1080/01434632.2019.1571073.

Gao, Yihong, Zengyan Jia, and Yan Zhou. 2015. EFL learning and identity development: A longitudinal study in 5 universities in China. *Journal of Language, Identity and Education* 14 (3): 137–158. https://doi.org/10.1080/15348458.2015.1041338.

Gaventa, John, and Rrajesh Tandon. 2010. *Globalizing citizens: New dynamics of inclusion and exclusion*. London: Zed Books Ltd.

Giddens, Anthony. 2006. Modernity and self-identity: Tribulations of the self. In *The discourse reader*, ed. Jaworski Adam and Nikolas Coupland, 415–427. London: Routledge.

Hegel, Georg Wilhelm Friedrich. 1977. *Phenomenology of spirit*. Translated by Arnold Vincent Miller. Oxford: Oxford University Press.

Jensen, Lene Arnett. 2021. Globalization: Human development in a new cultural context. In Joan Y. Chiao, Shu-Chen Li, Robert Turner, Su Yeon Lee-Tauler, and Beverly Pringle (eds.) *Oxford Handbook of cultural neuroscience and global mental health*. https://doi.org/10.1093/oxfordhb/9780190057695.013.24

Kamyab, Shahrzad, and Rosalind Latiner Raby. 2023. Introduction. In *Unintended consequences of internationalization in higher education: Comparative international perspectives on the impacts of policy and practice*, ed. Shahrzad Kamyab and Rosalind Latiner Raby, 27–33. New York: Routledge. https://doi.org/10.4324/9781003189916.

Kant, Immanuel. 1957. *Perpetual peace*. Edited by Lewis White Beck. Englewood Cliffs: Macmillan.

Kant, Immanuel. 1978. *Critique of practical reason*. Translated by Lewis White Beck. Indianapolis: Bobbs-Merrill.

Kant, Immanuel. 2002. *Groundwork of the metaphysics of morals*. Translated by Allen W. Wood. New Haven: Yale University Press.

Kant, Immanuel. 2007. Idea for a universal history with a cosmopolitan aim. In *Anthropology, history, and education*, ed. Günter. Zöller and Robert B. Louden, 107–120. Cambridge: Cambridge University Press.

Kleingeld, Pauline. 1998. Kant's cosmopolitan law: World citizenship for a global order. *Kantian Review* 2: 72–90. https://doi.org/10.1017/S1369415400000200.

Kleingeld, Pauline. 2012. *Kant and cosmopolitanism: The philosophical ideal of world citizenship*. Cambridge: Cambridge University Press. https://doi.org/10.1017/CBO9781139015486.

Mantero, Miguel. 2007. Toward ecological pedagogy in language education. In *Identity and second language learning: Culture, inquiry, and dialogic activity in educational contexts*, ed. Miguel Mantero, 1–11. Charlotte: Information Age Publishing.

Markus, Hazel R., and Paula Nurius. 1986. Possible selves. *American Psychologist* 41: 954–969.

MEXT. 2011. *Five proposals to improve the proficiency of English as lingua franca*. Retrieved 5 April 2023, from https://www.mext.go.jp/component/english/__icsFiles/afieldfile/2012/07/09/1319707_1.pdf

Mohammadi, Ariana N. 2022. Swearing in a second language: The role of emotions and perceptions. *Journal of Multilingual and Multicultural Development* 43 (7): 629–646.

National Curriculum Information Center. n.d. *Education system of Korea*. Retrieved 5 April 2024, from http://ncic.re.kr/english.inf.ivi.index.do

Oxford University Press. 2024. Morality. In *Oxford learner's dictionaries*. Retrieved 6 February 2024, from https://www.oxfordlearnersdictionaries.com/

Ricento, Thomas. 2005. Considerations of identity in L2 learning. In *Handbook of research in second language teaching and learning*, ed. Eli Hinkel, 895–910. New York: Routledge.

Riley, Philip. 2006. Self-expression and the negotiation of identity in a foreign language. *International Journal of Applied Linguistics* 16 (3): 295–318. https://doi.org/10.1111/j.1473-4192.2006.00120.x.

Rokita-Jaśkow, Joanna, and Dorota Werbińska. 2023. Language teacher identity and emotions in a duo ethnographic narrative: The perspective of teacher, parent, and teacher educator. *Theory and Practice of Second Language Acquisition* 9 (2): 1–26. https://doi.org/10.31261/TAPSLA.12686.

Roldán, Concha. 2018. The thinning and deformation of ethical and political concepts in the era of globalization. In *Philosophy of globalization*, ed. Concha Roldán, Daniel Brauer, and Johannes Rohbeck, 109–122. Berlin and Boston: Walter de Gruyter. https://doi.org/10.1515/9783110492415-009.

Rutgers, Dieuwerke, Michael Evans, Linda Fisher, Karen Forbes, Angela Gayton, and Yongcan Liu. 2024. Multilingualism, multilingual identity and academic attainment: Evidence from secondary schools in England. *Journal of Language, Identity and Education* 23 (2): 210–227. https://doi.org/10.1080/15348458.2021.1986397.

Sahakyan, Taguhi, Martin Lamb, and Gary Chambers. 2018. Language teacher motivation: From the ideal to the feasible self. In *Language teacher psychology*, ed. Sarah Mercer and Achilleas Kostoulas, 53–70. Bristol, Blue Ridge Summit: Multilingual Matters. https://doi.org/10.21832/9781783099467.

Sun, Xiaoan. 2020. Towards a common framework for global citizenship education: A critical review of UNESCO's conceptual framework of global citizenship education. In *Education and mobilities, perspectives on rethinking and reforming education*, ed. Xudong Zhu, Jiayong Li, Mang Li, Qiang Liu, and Hugh Starkey, 263–277. Singapore: Springer Nature. https://doi.org/10.1007/978-981-13-9031-9_15.

Sun, Tingting, and Adcharawan Buripakdi. 2021. Scrutiny of global citizenship in Chinese elementary school English textbooks and teachers' practices during COVID-19 pandemic. *Asia Pacific Journal of Educators and Education* 36 (2): 257–280. https://doi.org/10.21315/apjee2021.36.2.13.

Sung, Chit Cheung Matthew. 2020. Investing in English-mediated practices in the EMI university: The case of cross-border mainland Chinese students in Hong Kong. *Lingua* 243: 102919. https://doi.org/10.1016/j.lingua.2020.102919.

Taylor, Florentina, Vera Busse, Lubina Gagova, Emma Marsden, and Barbara Rooskén. 2013. *Identity in foreign language learning and teaching: Why listening to our students' and teachers' voices really matters*. London: British Council.

Torres, Carlos Alberto, and Emiliano Bosio. 2020. Global citizenship education at the crossroads: Globalization, global commons, common good, and critical consciousness. *Prospects* 48: 99–113. https://doi.org/10.1007/s11125-019-09458-w.

UNESCO. 2015. *Global citizenship education: Topics and learning objectives.* Paris: UNESCO.

Wang, Ying. 2021. Authenticity of identity and second language learning. *SAGE Open* 11 (4): 21582440211068516. https://doi.org/10.1177/215824402 1106851.

Wu, Manfred Man-fat. 2020. Second language teaching for global citizenship. *Globalisation, Societies and Education* 18 (3): 330–342. https://doi.org/10. 1080/14767724.2019.1693349.

Wu, Manfred Man-fat. 2023. *Sublating second language research and practices: Contribution from the Hegelian perspective.* London: Routledge.

Wu, Manfred Man-fat. 2024. Missing links in L2 teaching approaches in the context of globalisation. In *Progress in Education*, vol. 78, ed. Robert V. Nata, 69–94. New York: Nova Science.

Yuan, Rui, and Pauline Mak. 2018. Reflective learning and identity construction in practice, discourse and activity: Experiences of pre-service language teachers in Hong Kong. *Teaching and Teacher Education* 74: 205–214. https://doi. org/10.1016/j.tate.2018.05.009.

PART II

Globalisation's Impacts and Inadequacies

CHAPTER 2

Opportunities and Challenges for Globalised L2 Identity

Abstract This chapter identifies the opportunities and challenges for second language (L2) identity brought by globalisation. The opportunities identified are English classroom as an ideal niche for global identity construction, fluid and flexible post-structural identity, and material benefits. The challenges include globalisation's neglect of individual subjectivity, the rise of nationalism, homogenisation of culture, and naïve cosmopolitanism. To maximise the opportunities and minimise the negative effects of globalisation, the following measures are proposed: Inclusion of human rights and duties to others into L2 teaching; provision of expression of voice for learners for cultural alternatives; inclusion of writer identity in the L2 writing curriculum; grammar teaching for the construction of globalised L2 identity; and finally, the provision of a more balanced description of English native-speaking cultures and those of other cultures in L2 textbooks.

Keywords Globalisation · L2 identity · Nationalism · Human rights · L2 writer identity · Globalised L2 identity

© The Author(s), under exclusive license to Springer Nature
Switzerland AG 2024
M. M. Wu, *Globalisation and Second Language Identity*,
https://doi.org/10.1007/978-3-031-68248-3_2

21

INTRODUCTION

Despite the increasing attention given to how globalisation influences L2 teaching, there have been a lack of discussions on how L2 identity is influenced by globalisation. This chapter aims to ameliorate the lack of attention given to this area by proposing how the implementation of L2 identity can maximise the potential and overcome the challenges of globalisation on the development and maintenance of L2 identity.

As described in Chapter 1, Kant's conceptualisation of globalisation has a solid foundation in his philosophical system, and the concept of global citizenship is similar to Kant's idea of a "kingdom of ends", which is based on his moral philosophy as given in his *Critique of practical reason* (Kant 1978) and *Groundwork of the metaphysics of morals* (Kant 2002). Kant's global theory continues to exert considerable influences on research and discussions on globalisation to date (e.g., Browning 2011). As stated by Browning (2011), "[C]ontemporary global theory, in many of its idioms, follows Kant in taking the interactions of human beings in time and space to culminate in a global identity" (37).

There have been burgeoning discussions on applying Kant's notion of global citizenship to the education field. For example, Hansen (2008) offers the idea of cosmopolitan inheritance, which according to him can cultivate students' cosmopolitan sensibility. Cosmopolitan sensibility consists of respect for and recognition of other cultures. It is a quality that can broaden students' creative and ethical horizons as well as develop their sense of hospitality. According to Kant, cosmopolitan law regulates interactions between individual citizens and non-citizens (Kleingeld 1998, 2012), and language plays an important role in the interactions. In interacting effectively with non-citizens abroad, or in Kant's words, fellow citizens of the earth, individuals have to be competent in a language that can be understood by the non-citizens (Council of Europe 2001). The English language, which enjoys the privilege of a lingua franca on the global level, is the best candidate for realising the notion of global citizenship, i.e., protecting the cosmopolitan right of all world citizens and enforcing cosmopolitan law. More importantly, the incorporation of cosmopolitan sensibility, cosmopolitan rights, and hospitality right into L2 identity enables L2 learners to become members contributing positively to the globalised world.

Kleingeld (1998, 2012) argues that in addition to interactions, the right to hospitality is another key element of cosmopolitan law.

Cosmopolitan law is based on the principle of refusal of entry by foreigners when they are likely to cause destruction to the people and physical environment of a nation. Again, the use of foreign languages is inevitable in the protection of this hospitality right, and L2 identity, which affects how learners perceive themselves as L2 learners and users, plays a critical role in their observation of the cosmopolitan law. Given the importance of language in the achievement of global citizenship, the language classroom is the ideal venue for the promotion of global citizenship (Wu 2020). After learning an L2, learners can put into practice what they have learned in the classroom to create a more peaceful and hospitable world.

In his *Idea of a universal history on a cosmopolitical plan* (Kant 2007), Kant provides nine propositions on his account on the natural development of a cosmopolitic state and world order. In his first four propositions Kant expresses that the teleological nature of human beings is part of nature, and the realisation of natural purpose is applicable to other animal species but not to individuals. Reasoning is the unique feature of humans, and there is an asocial tendency of humans. Foreign language learning facilitates the development of human reasoning and the natural plan of a cosmopolitic state be realised. Kant (2007) begins to discuss cosmopolitanism and global citizenship in the fifth proposition, that human beings have a natural tendency to establish a civil society (proposition five) and are in need of a master (proposition six). There is also a need for international relations adjusted to laws between states (proposition seven), and the development of a perfect state or civil society, including its internal and external relations, can be regarded as the realisation of a plan of nature (proposition eight). The operation of international relations cannot take place without the use of foreign languages, and L2 identity exerts influences on the learning and use of foreign languages. It is only in this naturally developed state that individuals can develop their potential to the fullest extent (proposition nine).

Kant did not provide details on the implementation of his plan described above. However, from the above account it can be implied that foreign languages have an important role to play in the realisation of nature's plan of civil society (Commission of the European Communities 2003; Liakhovska 2021), and L2 identity has unique functions to perform in this endeavour.

In the realisation of the natural plan of cosmopolitic state, the protection of rights and promotion of global citizenship by Kant, there are opportunities and challenges for L2 identity. The discussions in this chapter are driven by the following three questions:

(a) What are the opportunities globalisation has brought for L2 identity?
(b) What are the challenges globalisation has brought to L2 identity?
(c) What are the ways for maximising the opportunities and overcoming the challenges described in 'a' and 'b'?

In the remainder of this chapter, discussions on the opportunities and challenges to L2 identity globalisation has brought, and proposals for maximising the potential for globalised L2 identity and overcoming the challenges to L2 identity are offered. They are followed by proposed means for achieving the above two aims.

OPPORTUNITIES FOR L2 IDENTITY IN THE GLOBALISATION CONTEXT

Globalisation has substantially transformed the nature of L2 learning (see, for example, Benson and Lamb 2020), including the creation of new opportunities for L2 learners. Prominent opportunities are introduced below.

Opportunity 1—English Classroom as an Ideal Niche for Global Identity Development

As briefly described in the introductory section of this chapter, the L2 classroom is a good location for global citizenship education (GCE) for both instrumental and educational reasons (Jakubiak 2020). In most existing L2 curricula, provisions are given to the needs of specific user groups from different cultural backgrounds (e.g., Illés 2012). The individualistic and personalised nature of the Communicative Language Teaching approach (Ho 2020) is also highly facilitative to the teaching of global citizenship. The importance of language as a marker for group membership, means of communication, and therefore identity construction, has been widely recognised (e.g., Zhang 2022). Wu (2020) has already shown how Kant's cosmopolitan and hospitality rights can be fostered as parts of L2 identity in the L2 classroom, and Wu et al. (In press) have explained how English as an international language can be used for global citizenship education. Kuwaiti students in universities who used English were found to embrace a global identity more than those who did not (Hasanen et al. 2014). Chen (2022) reports the empirical findings of students becoming more accepting of non-native varieties of English and more confident as users of English after being taught Global Englishes based pedagogy. The increase in self-efficacy as English users confirmed the earlier findings of Ke (2016) as well as Sert and Özkan (2020). The conclusion is that the English language facilitated the development of a global identity.

Cabrera (2010) proposes the cultivation of positive valuation, empathy, perspective-taking, and altruism of learners as the key elements in GCE. Among these elements, the positive effects of perspective-taking have received empirical support. Perspective-taking was recommended by Illés (2012) for cultivation of a reconceptualised L2 autonomy demanded by globalisation. Cabrera (2010) promotes trans-border activities for primary and secondary school students and trans-border service learning for GCE, with English being used as a lingua franca in these activities. What is common to these proposals is that the use of a common language is essential. Again, English would be a choice for communication for most parties who do not share a common language. These proposals resonate with Hansen's (2008) advocacy for cosmopolitan sensibility with the two elements of respect for and recognition of other cultures. The cultivation of elements such as perspective-taking and cosmopolitan sensibility into L2 identity can facilitate positive L2 identity development and harness learners' prowess to overcome the challenges caused by globalisation such as misunderstandings and prejudice caused by lack of respect and recognition of other cultures. The L2 classroom is an ideal venue for cultivating these qualities.

Opportunity 2—Fluid and Flexible Post-structural Identity

L2 identity is one of the key learner variables having been researched for decades. Since its emergence as a research field, its research has been dominated by psychosocial perspectives. A "social turn" in the L2 research field (Block 2003; Dörnyei and Ushioda 2011) has resulted in a heightened awareness of the social influences on L2 identity, with some notable theories such as Norton's (2001) imagined communities, an ideal community that learners pursue to engage in, or a set of imagined identities that influences a learner's investment in their L2 learning. According to Norton (Norton and Pavlenko 2019), imagined communities affect the following aspects of L2 learning: learning trajectories, motivation, and resistance. The term imagined community was originally coined by Anderson (1991) referring to nationality, with subsequent research conducted by Dagenais et al. (2008) on children's imagined community of their neighbourhood in Canada, and Kendrick and Jones (2008) on the perception of imagined communities of Uganda aroused by pictures and drawing. The extension of the post-structuralist approaches to L2 learning concurs with the stance of a fluid and flexible view of L2 identity adopted in this book.

Globalisation is a powerful force that influences learners' motivation, choice of language, and ways of learning a foreign language (Block and Cameron 2002). According to Block and Cameron (2002), the emergence of terms such as hybridisation (Pieterse 1995) and glocalisation (Robertson 1995) describe the phenomenon of synthesis between local and foreign cultures. Attracting particular attention by researchers is glocalisation, which in the general sense refers to the co-occurrence of universalisation and particularisation tendencies in contemporary social, political, and economic systems simultaneously (Blatter 2022), and the merger of global and local perspectives on these aspects (Patel and Lynch 2013). Applying to the L2 context, it refers to the local adaptation of international educational approaches in English learning and teaching taking into consideration local culture and context (Pineda et al. 2022). The synthesis of foreign and local cultures due to globalisation has resulted in a fluid L2 identity. Individuals in the globalisation context possess a hybrid "bicultural identity" consisting of a local and a global identity, which very often cannot be distinguished from one another (Arnett 2002). The concept of hybrid identity has received empirical support from L2 researchers such as Henry and Goddard (2015) and Sung (2014).

One observation on the influences of globalisation is that in facing foreign novel cultures, individuals feel the foreignness of their own native culture, and therefore may gain a better understanding and loyalty to their own native cultures, for example, in the form of nationalism (Block and Cameron 2002; see also Dengler 2023). This demand for a fluid and flexible L2 identity equips learners with adaptability and enables them to benefit from multifarious and fast-changing cultural contexts they encounter (Choi 2018; Zhang and Guo 2015). According to Illés (2012), one important contextual change between the past situations and the contemporary globalised L2 learning context is that instead of having a lack of exposure to the target language, learners are facing the problem of plenty. Therefore, being able to communicate successfully in an international setting is a prerequisite for linguistic competence and this competence should be an integral part of L2 identity. Conventional L2 teaching, which emphasises training, is no longer sufficient for the ever-emerging new contexts. Since foreign languages are linguistic capital (Bourdieu 1991), the make-up of the linguistic capital is changing. Richards (2021) expressed that the Internet has resulted in new possibilities for learners to create identities not related to their physical selves. Thus, there can be multiplication of L2 identity across various cyber spaces.

Despite not focusing on L2 identity per se but on L2 autonomy, Illés (2012) points out that globalisation is characterised by "fluid and emergent contexts in which speakers from a variety of language and cultural backgrounds interact" (505). Because of this prominent feature of the contemporary L2 learning contexts, she calls for a negotiated approach for the promotion and implementation of L2 learning autonomy, alongside the use of literature and the use of translation in teaching. The use of literature and translation is also recommended by Choi (2018) and Wu (2016).

Opportunity 3—Material Benefits Brought by Globalisation

In the globalised world, foreign language learning experiences greater intensity of commodification and the link between language and cultural identity has become blurred. Gray (2002) lists three ways of how the English language is connected to globalisation. They are the growth of transnational corporations, the increasing number and influences of world organisations, and the increasing prevalence of the Internet. These three influences result in the increasing importance of English learning for individuals to benefit economically, socially, culturally, and politically from globalisation.

A greater variety of products and cheaper goods are available in the contemporary globalised world because of consumerism and global commercialisation (Zajda and Rust 2021). Globalisation also opens global communication that is vital to the world economy and population/ individual mobility. Faster delivery of consumer products is available worldwide via online shopping, and cheap and free entertainment, cheap travelling, and tourism have become popular (see also Tarozzi and Torres 2016).

With the exponential increase in the availability of electronic media, learners are able to enjoy innumerable entertainment and useful information in different forms unrestricted by time and space. The increasing number of electronic channels also means an explosion of opportunities for establishing businesses and investments for enhancing the material well-being of individuals. Despite the fact that globalisation brings material comfort, Giddens (2006) remarks that the so-called personalised needs are met by standardised products. As interpersonal interactions for mutual recognition, a key element of self-identity construction, and social bonding in Hegel's (1971; 1977; see also Wu 2016) anthro-political philosophy, are not involved in commodity consumption, the material conveniences do not contribute positively to identity construction.

Echoing the above benefits resulting from globalisation, L2 learners experience a sharp increase in their exposure to foreign languages (Benson and Lamb 2020), especially given the rapid development in digital communication technology. The ubiquity of communication technologies also provides learners with more choices in terms of the language to learn, learning modes, and pace. These ripples on L2 teaching in the classroom resonate with the first opportunity described above, at the same time raise the issue of the blurring boundaries between classroom and out-of-class L2 learning.

CHALLENGES TO L2 IDENTITY IN THE GLOBALISATION CONTEXT

As the title of this chapter and book suggests, apart from the opportunities available for L2 learners, L2 learners and teachers need to be aware of and to overcome certain challenges in relation to globalisation. Details are given below.

Challenge 1—Neglect of Individual Subjectivity

Globalisation has led to an emergence of managerialism which emphasises labour mobility and workforce training to accommodate globalisation

(McNamara 2019). The popularity of the Common European Framework for Reference for Languages (CEFR) (Council of Europe 2020) is a major response made by Europe to globalisation. The challenge caused by managerialism is the neglect of individual subjectivity. McNamara (2019) states that

> (W)hat is needed instead is to give an account of how language learning in different societies and cultures will have specific social meanings, and hence potential meanings for individuals, within the history of contact, culturally and politically, with the societies and communities in which the target language is spoken, and the resulting discourses involved (116).

The above neglect of individual subjectivity is a barrier to the development of a globalised L2 identity, as L2 identity comprises the subjectivities of individuals.

Another challenge related to the neglect of individual subjectivity is neoliberalism. Neoliberal ideas on the global connections being possessed by elites are at odds with the value of equality and justice (De Costa et al. 2021), the universal values upon which globalisation and global citizenship are based. The contradictions between elitism and equality and justice create dissonances for L2 identity. Estellés and Fischman (2020), adopting a critical perspective on GCE, viewed GCE as promoting neoliberal policies which promotes economic inequality and social injustices instead of positive universal values. Both language educators and learners should be informed of this contradiction.

Globalisation implies a growing interdependence between different parts of the world and their members (Illés 2012), and L2 learners and teachers should be informed of this. The subjectivity between themselves and others in interacting with others located in different parts of the world, or to echo Hansen (2008), with cosmopolitan sensibility as part of the L2 identity, is equally important. This is especially true given the neglect of individual subjectivity of globalisation.

Globalisation not only influences L2 identity but also the identity of learners' native language. Elliot and Lemert (2010) raise the issue of the emotional costs, an important element of subjectivity, of new individualism caused by globalisation, which has been receiving empirical support (e.g., Zhang and Semple 2016). According to them, globalisation has given rise to a new individualism characterised by a "reinvention craze", with examples of self-help, therapy, management restructurings, and corporate downsizings. The "reinvention craze" has created an endless hunger for instant change and self-reinvention for individuals and the emotional pressures it exerts on individuals is the cost individuals have to pay.

Challenge 2—Glocalisation and the Rise of Nationalism

Roudometof (2016) provides a critical introduction to the concept of glocalisation, including its origins, how it is related to globalisation and how it affects identities of the contemporary cosmopolitan era. Despite focusing on social identity rather than specifically on L2 identity, Roudometof's (2016) account offers some insights on this topic. According to him, the concept of glocalisation is theoretically underdeveloped, and to date there have been no attempts to theorise glocalisation on its own terms. He interpreted glocalisation as influencing identities of individuals through the effects of popular culture and consumer culture. On the other hand, glocalisation affects national identities and religious belonging. Roudometof's (2016) account indicates that L2 identities, as part of the general identities, are also under influences such as consumerism because of the material benefits and convenience globalisation has brought. These contradictory forces have repercussions on L2 identity.

Unlike Roudometof (2016), Mallinson (2021) expresses directly that the promotion of globalisation in the L2 classroom is at the same time a promotion of nationalism, which creates tensions for L2 learners. According to him, L2 experts such as Brown (1993) view that the teaching of internationalisation in Japanese classrooms has resulted in a kind of superficial internationalisation which is counter-productive to the development of a globalised L2 identity of learners, or naïve cosmopolitanism to be described below. Liang (2015) reports the Japanese government's hesitation in promoting the English language for fear of its threat to the Japanese language and Japanese identity. For McNamara (2019) and Dengler (2023), there has been a shift to an increasing emphasis on nationalism in the theoretical development of the study of language. An example McNamara (2019) gave was the upsurge of nationalism in Australia upon the establishment of the first socialist government in 1972. Dengler (2023), on the other hand, advocates for "a return to nationalism", meaning to localise English language teaching to counterbalance the Western hegemonic ideology which is detrimental to the healthy development of a globalised L2 identity. The difficulties Asian learners of English face in maintaining a sense of national identity in globalisation, particularly with the use of English as a lingua franca (Feng and Wang 2020), and South Korean students' belief that participation in global citizenship requiring a native competence of English and that it is a threat to their Korean identity (Cavanagh 2020) are also good examples of the tensions between globalisation and nationalism.

Challenge 3—Homogenisation of Cultures

Galloway and Rose (2015) focus on the challenge of homogenisation of cultures initiated by globalisation. McNamara (2019) comments that the promotion of English as an international language is hegemonic, as it involves an "imposition of a single set of cultural meanings and social and political values for language education" (117). The hegemonic imposition of English as an international language inevitably thwarts the healthy development of a globalised L2 identity, as it promotes cultural relativism. The homogenisation of education policies, including language policies, across nations (Benson 2006), may cause undesirable effects such as the adoption of native speaker standards for L2 teaching and assessments.

Globalisation has been regarded as the origin of language death (extinction) and linguistic imperialism (see Galloway and Rose 2015). These two phenomena undoubtedly exert negative influences on L2 identity as cultural pluralism is threatened. There is also a loss of relevance of local forms of government of nation states which takes into consideration local culture (Demuth 2018). Given this, the promotion of cosmopolitan right, hospitality right, and cosmopolitan sensibility (as pointed out in Chapter 1 and this chapter) not only to L2 learners but native speakers of English is essential.

Challenge 4—Naïve Cosmopolitanism

Golding (2017) warns against the danger of "naïve cosmopolitanism" that treats Kant's theories as impartial and universal. This view echoes a prevalent view that the Kantian perspective is culturally biased on the Western concept of Enlightenment and excludes the role of "the Other" in the L2 classroom, and thus brings undesirable influences on L2 identity. Golding (2017) suggests the concept of "border cosmopolitanism" developed by Mignolo (2000), which takes into consideration local contexts, empowerment of participants, and application of this approach based on the critical pedagogy of Paolo Freire (1970).

As its name suggests, border cosmopolitanism adopts a critical stance on the Eurocentric historical and theoretical roots of cosmopolitanism and provides "a theoretical foundation for a decolonising cosmopolitanism" (Golding 2017: 7). The outcome of employing the problem-posing education for border cosmopolitanism, according to Golding, "might resemble a dialogue between the hegemonic values that inform secular cosmopolitan ethics, such as democracy, rights and citizenship, and local ways of knowing that have been historically subordinated to such values" (Golding 2017: 15). Golding (2017) also remarks that a critique of cosmopolitan discourses by border cosmopolitanism can result in a language for empowerment, which is beneficial to L2 identity development. Despite efforts by scholars such as Golding, theoretical lacunae such as the extent and form of synthesis between global and local culture (Robertson 1995) still remain to be filled.

PROPOSALS FOR OPPORTUNITIES AND CHALLENGES CAUSED BY GLOBALISATION

To maximise the opportunities and minimise the negative effects of globalisation, this book proposes several measures, and details are given below.

Highlighting Human Rights and Duties to Others

In line with the stance of this book, it is recommended that rights be incorporated into L2 teaching to develop learners' globalised L2 identity (Sun 2020). The incorporation of rights into L2 teaching will enable L2 learners to perform optimally in the economic, social, and political realms. The concept of universal right, which views individuals as an end, should be introduced to L2 learners and teachers. They should also be informed about how the concept of universal hospitality forms the basis for cosmopolitan public rights, a system of law for people on cosmopolitanism. Two types of rights in Kant's philosophy, namely, cosmopolitan rights and hospitality rights, have already been proposed to be incorporated into the L2 curriculum (Wu 2020). Lazos (2018) argues that despite Kant's support for federalism, his work *Perpetual peace* (Kant 1957) indicates that Kant favoured the legalisation of hospitality right.

Foreigners should be legally protected to safeguard human autonomy, and this principle should be anti-xenophobic, foreigner-friendly, and anti-colonial in nature. These initiatives can equip learners with the capacity to cope with the linguistic and schematic diversity they face in the globalised L2 learning context (Illés 2012).

Shani (2003) emphasises the need for the development of a global political culture based on human rights. He offers the possible factors that contribute to the failure of the liberal project to achieve multiple identities in the globalisation context: The incommensurability of cultural value systems; the dynamism of modernity; and distortions originated from pre-modern practices. Supranational centres of regulation such as the World Trade Organization and International Monetary Fund should play a key role in mediating regional conflicts and ensuring global justice in which all fundamental rights should be guaranteed for all persons (Di Castro 2018). Equally important is the implementation of initiatives by these supranational centres to alleviate the negative outcomes of neoliberalism, for example, through redistributing resources on education on a global basis and international agreements on trade. However, since Shani (2003) introduced his suggestion two decades ago, few developments have been made in this area.

Globalisation has resulted in a need for morality (Wu 2020; Wu et al. in press), and the conventional concept of remedial duties, which are obligations for individuals to aid those who are in need, is no longer applicable in the contemporary globalised era (Rohbeck 2018). The concept of remedial duties is based on local communities, and it needs to be replaced by duties based on the global community, i.e., globalised remedial duties. Rohbeck (2018) contends that there has been an exacerbation of inequalities caused by globalisation, and this was partly due to historical trends such as colonisation. Therefore, he proposes that both positive (i.e., globalised remedial duties) and negative (avoiding doing harm to other parts of the world) moral duties to play commensurate roles. According to this proposal, these two types of duties should be taken into consideration in facilitating the L2 identity of learners. This proposal can enhance learners' respect for and recognition of other cultures, thus preventing the challenges of nationalism, cultural relativism, and homogenisation of culture.

The recent resurgence in interest in Kant's cosmopolitanism is not only found in the academic field but also in the realisation of cosmopolitanism among human rights and peace organisations such as the United Nations and the Criminal Court (Hansen 2008). In his evaluation of the extent to which the European Union (EU) realised Kant's model of cosmopolitan federation of states, Brown (2014) comments that the EU failed badly in respect of Kant's cosmopolitan right as stated in Kant's Third Definitive Article of his *Perpetual peace*. This failure reflects a strong need for not only the EU but nations across the globe to further develop this aspect.

Provision of Expression of Voice for Learners

Pennycook (1997) argues for the expression of voice by learners for cultural alternatives in the achievement of autonomy. This concept is intimately related to L2 identity because in Kant's (2002) view a morally autonomous person observes rules and laws on a voluntary basis. Autonomy has become a global discourse that is regarded as a universal positive trait, and Kant (e.g., 2002) treats autonomy as the basis of human dignity, the source of all morality, and the highest stage of moral development. The mainstream views ignore the communitarian aspect of autonomy which takes into consideration the rights of others.

At the same time, Pennycook (1997) remarked that the concept of autonomy is bound by Western culture, and that different cultures have different conceptualisations of learner autonomy. His conclusion is that there is a strong need for learners to be empowered to find means to articulate their meanings that are embedded in their cultures and contexts, and teachers should play an active role in facilitating learners to find a "voice" or cultural alternatives. The deprivation of learners' space for expressing their non-native identities because of Englishisation of higher education worldwide, an outcome of globalisation, has been documented (Wang 2020). The opportunity for the expression of voice enables learners to construct a fluid and flexible post-structural L2 identity and overcome the pitfalls caused by globalisation's neglect for individual subjectivity (Choi 2018) described earlier in this chapter.

While the expression of voice is important, awareness and knowledge of different varieties of English ("other voices") as opposed to "standard English" only is equally important (Illés 2012). Language teachers need to inform learners that audience in the globalised world

> do not represent a homogeneous group but are made up of speakers of different languages with a variety of cultural backgrounds, which makes

accommodating the demands of such a diverse group of people even more difficult (Illés 2012: 511).

The above view highly resembles Norton's (Norton and Pavlenko 2019) idea of imagined communities introduced earlier. The empirical results of Salih and Omar's (2021) research on a cross-cultural project between Omani undergraduates and their American counterparts indicate the importance and feasibility of achieving higher level of acceptance on intercultural differences.

The provision of voice for learners and the remaining proposals below enable the maximum use of the L2 classroom for cultivating positive L2 identity. The provision of voice for learners also overcomes the four challenges described in the previous section by focusing on the individuality of learners.

Inclusion of Writer Identity in the L2 Writing Curriculum

The inclusion of writer identity in the writing curriculum for learners who are mature enough to understand the abstract concept of L2 identity has been proposed (Jones and Beck 2020). Working on writer identity can raise learners' awareness and sensitivity to how L2 writing contributes to and transforms their L2 identity. It also raises learners' awareness of how their own life histories influence their L2 identity. As with the expression of voice mentioned above, this inclusion of writer L2 identity enables learners to benefit from the opportunity to construct a fluid and flexible post-structural identity. This is because learners' personal, social, and political awareness are augmented through these reflective activities. Little (2007) recommends using a learner journal, which is an effective means for recording the development of L2 identity over time.

On the interpersonal aspect,

> [t]he construction of a writer's discoursal self is mediated by social interaction. That is, the actual writer-reader relationship in which an act of writing is embedded influences how writers portray themselves through their discoursal choice ... The discoursal resources out of which writers construct their discoursal self are the product of actual intertextual (in Vygotsky's term, 'inter-mental') encounters in the writer's life history (Ivanič 1998: 328).

Ivanič (1998) is one of the early precursors of a discursive approach to the study of L2 identity. Gee (2003) distinguishes between primary and secondary Discourses and regards both types of Discourses as important in the construction of L2 identity. Primary Discourses are prevalent in daily life, which according to Gee (2003) construct our first social identity, the basis for the subsequent development of identity. Secondary Discourses, on the other hand, are specialised discourses of knowledge and abstractions, often the only aspect emphasised in literacy training. The main focuses of his framework are intersubjectivity, negotiation of meaning, power, struggles, and challenges of dominant ideologies. Gee's (2003) framework is highly suitable for the discursive approach to L2 identity research. It can also foster globalised L2 identity because its focuses are perennial issues involved in globalisation thus empowers L2 learners to overcome the relevant challenges.

Another exploration of L2 identity from a discoursal perspective was undertaken by Hirano (2009). In this study, qualitative data were collected from classroom interactions, interviews, and diaries of learners, teachers, and researchers. Findings indicate that discursive interactions shape L2 identity, and learner difficulty is related to their L2 identity. Given the premise that L2 identities are amenable to change, Hirano (2009) advises teachers to focus on the development of learners' competence and the context of text production. Richards (2006) adopts Zimmerman's (1998) model of discoursal and social identities which distinguishes between discourse, as well as situated and transportable identities. According to him, transportable identities, which are latent and can be invoked during interaction, are the key to research on motivation because they can stimulate personal involvement. Transportable identities are highly relevant to L2 identity in the context of globalisation, as globalisation places unprecedented demands on individuals in terms of their autonomy and fluidity of L2 identity. Again, these concepts on identity are powerful tools for L2 learners for overcoming the challenges caused by globalisation.

Grammar Teaching for Construction of Globalised L2 Identity

A less commonly recognised aspect of how L2 teaching contributes to the construction of globalised L2 identity is that L2 grammar learning transforms learners' identities. In learning L2 grammar, learners will discover that grammatical rules are universal in nature. At the same time, their awareness of the similarities and differences in the grammar and language of English-speaking and other cultures will be raised through L2 grammar learning. This means that L2 grammar learning broadens individuals' horizons. Grammar, which is often treated as static rules containing universals, is in fact dynamic and contributes to the formation of L2 identity. Soruç and Griffiths (2015) found empirical evidence of negative interferences to L2 identity in learning the spoken grammar of a foreign language.

Grammar learning also broadens the universal forms of language for L2 learners and forces them to reflect on the grammar of their native language. Through comparison with the grammatical rules of their own native language, L2 learners are able to learn more about their own native language. With additional forms of language, especially with the need for foreign language learning caused by globalisation, L2 learners inevitably have their identities transformed into more fluid and flexible post-structural ones.

Another relatively unnoticed area is that L2 identities are affected by intonation, and the teaching of intonation can result in positive changes to learner identity (Morgan 1997). The positive changes were achieved by language teachers designing and implementing pedagogy on sentence-level stress and intonation with practice content challenging learner assumptions such as gender inequality. These types of research can increase our understanding of how positive L2 identity development can be nurtured.

Provision of a More Balanced Description of English Native-Speaking Cultures and Inclusion of Other Cultures in L2 Textbooks

To date, the contents of many L2 textbooks are heavily biased towards the English native-speaking cultures and lack a global dimension (see, for example, Dengler 2023; Risager 2018; Rose and Galloway 2019; Sifakis 2014). In their analysis of English textbooks in Germany, Syrbe and Rose (2018) concluded that there is an over-reliance of UK models, and the descriptions of language users and cultures in these textbooks are static in nature. This finding shows that there is a substantial gap between the proposed enhancements for theoretical development, research, and practice in L2 identity to cope with the ever-expanding and evolving trend of globalisation. A similar finding is reported from an earlier textbook analysis, that cultures of the Inner Circle (Kachru 1985) dominate the content of seven series of English teaching textbooks (Shin et al. 2011). In Kachru's (1985) concentric circle model on the variety of English, the inner circle comprises countries such as Britain, the US, Australia, Canada, and New Zealand, in which English is used as a native language among people. The outer circle mainly includes former colonies of the British Empire, such as India, Malaysia, Singapore, Ghana, and Kenya. Finally, the expanding circle refers to countries that treat English as a means of communication with the inner and outer circles, with countries such as China, Turkey, Japan, and Korea.

Song (2013) has identified a similar trend of the dominance of the cultures of Inner Circle in English textbooks in the Korean context. The same trend was identified by Davidson and Liu (2020), that the simplistic representations of culture in Japanese elementary school English textbook create barriers for global education. Xu (2013), on the other hand, found advancements in including cultures other than English in addition to English-speaking cultures in secondary level English textbooks in China. Dengler (2023) concurs with Sun and Buripakdi (2023) and proposes localisation and integration of national contents in ELT materials and textbooks to create opportunities for learners to express their own cultural backgrounds and lived experiences. The provision of a more balanced description of native and non-native cultures in textbooks enables the construction of a fluid and flexible globalised L2 identity for learners and can minimise the negative effects of homogenisation of culture.

The conclusion given by Dengler (2023) serves as an excellent remark on this issue:

> For ELT in Laos and other contexts in the Global South, a return to the nation by the inclusion of national content and references present an opportunity to counterbalance the hegemonic power of 'international' or 'global' English and coloniality in today's English teaching and learning (p. 330).

This proposal facilitates the construction of L2 identity to overcome the challenges of the rise of nationalism, homogenisation of cultures, and naïve cosmopolitanism through emphasising pluriculturism.

CONCLUSION

Judging from the above accounts of globalisation in the literature on L2 identity, the personal reflective and social interactive aspects of Kant's philosophy have been put forward by L2 experts despite not being explicitly stated, as indicated by proposals two and three of this chapter. However, the aspect of right, which is the building block of Kant's theory of global citizenship, needs to be reinforced in fostering L2 identity in the globalised context (Wu 2020). In addition to raising L2 learners' awareness on their right to cosmopolitanism and hospitality, equally important is to make them aware that equal right also belongs to members of humanity all over the globe, and they have the commensurate obligations of ensuring the rights of all other individual on earth are well protected and enforced. The awareness raising of L2 learners, as pointed out by Kant, enables the establishment of a civil society and harmonious inter-state relations, which are the realisation of plans of nature. The realisation of plans of nature can ultimately allow individuals to fully develop their potential as Kant (1957, 2007) envisaged.

Citing Jacobson (2001) and Kaldor (2003), Shani (2003) is of the view that

> David Jacobson speaks for many when he writes that what 'we are witnessing is the development of a global (if still limited to the northern hemisphere) political culture based on human rights – which is demarcated (in principle) in non-territorial terms and, in its domain, is distinct from territorial states (the local political authorities)' (Jacobson, 2001, p. 177). Mary Kaldor is more emphatic in her assertion that horizontal transnational networks are replacing vertical territorial based forms of civil society on a global scale (38).

This chapter has offered a snapshot of selected opportunities and challenges of globalisation for L2 identity which the author deems a priority. Other challenges such as global health, global environment, and global climatic hazards which increasingly affect the world population also deserve attention. There should be more discussions on how these emerging phenomena influence L2 identity.

REFERENCES

Arnett, Jeffrey Jensen. 2002. The psychology of globalization. *American Psychologist* 57: 774–783. https://doi.org/10.1037/0003-066X.57.10.774.

Benson, Phil. 2006. Autonomy in language teaching and learning. *Language Teaching* 40: 21–40. https://doi.org/10.1017/S0261444806003958.

Benson, Phil and Lamb, Terry. 2020. Autonomy in the age of multilingualism. In Manuel Jimenez Raya and Flavia Vieira (eds.) *Autonomy in language education: Theory, research and practice*, 74–88. New York and London: Routledge. https://doi.org/10.4324/9780429261336-7

Blatter, Joachim. Glocalization. *Encyclopedia Britannica*, 23 Feb. 2022, Retrieved 2 April 2024, from https://www.britannica.com/money/glocalization

Block, David. 2003. *The social turn in second language acquisition*. Edinburgh: Edinburgh University Press. https://doi.org/10.3366/j.ctvxcrwd8

Block, David and Cameron, Deborah. 2002. Introduction. In David Block and Deborah Cameron (eds.) *Globalization and language teaching*, 1–10. London: Routledge. https://doi.org/10.4324/9780203193679

Bourdieu, Pierre. 1991. *Language and symbolic power*. Translated by Gino Raymond and Matthew Adamson. Cambridge: Polity Press.

Brown, Derek. 1993. February. Getting beyond the internationalization cliche. *JET Journal* 1993: 80–85.

Brown, Garrett Wallace. 2014. The European Union and Kant's idea of cosmopolitan right: Why the EU is not cosmopolitan. *European Journal of International Relations* 20 (3): 671–693. https://doi.org/10.1177/135406 6113482991.

Browning, Gary. 2011. *Global theory from Kant to Hardt and Negri*. Basingstoke: Palgrave Macmillan.

Cabrera, Luis. 2010. *The practice of global citizenship*. Cambridge: Cambridge University Press. https://doi.org/10.1017/CBO9780511762833.

Cavanagh, Claire. 2020. The role of English in global citizenship. *Journal of Global Citizenship & Equity Education* 7 (1): 1–23. https://doi.org/10. 13140/RG.2.2.21671.60328.

Chen, Rainbow Tsai-Hung. 2022. Effects of Global Englishes-oriented pedagogy in the EFL classroom. *System* 111: 102946. https://doi.org/10.1016/j.system.2022.102946.

Choi, Lee Jin. 2018. Embracing identities in second language learning: Current status and future directions. *Problems of Education in the 21st Century* 76 (6): 800–815. https://doi.org/10.33225/pec/18.76.800

Commission of the European Communities. 2003. *Promoting language learning and linguistic diversity: An action plan 2004–2006*. Brussels: Commission of the European Communities.

Council of Europe. 2020. *Common European Framework of Reference for Languages: Learning, teaching, assessment—Companion volume.* Strasbourg: Council of Europe Publishing.

Davidson, Rachel, and Yongcan Liu. 2020. Reaching the world outside: Cultural representation and perceptions of global citizenship in Japanese elementary school English textbooks. *Language, Culture and Curriculum* 33 (1): 32–49. https://doi.org/10.1080/07908318.2018.1560460.

De Costa, Peter I., Green-Eneix, Curtis and Li, Wenjing (Wendy). 2021. Embracing diversity, inclusion, equity and access in EMI-TNHE: Towards a social justice-centered reframing of English language teaching. *RELC Journal* 52 (2): 227–235. https://doi.org/10.1177/00336882211018540

Demuth, Constanze. 2018. Liberalism's all-inclusive promise of freedom and its illiberal effects: A critique of the concept of globalization. In Concha Roldán, Daniel Brauer, and Johannes Rohbeck (eds.) *Philosophy of globalization,* 63–77. Berlin and Boston: Walter de Gruyter. https://doi.org/10.1515/978311 0492415

Dengler, Rebecca. 2023. Global or local?—Notions of nationalism and coloniality in ELT material. *Language and Intercultural Communication* 23 (3): 321–332. https://doi.org/10.1080/14708477.2023.2196262.

Di Castro, Elisabetta. 2018. Globalization, inequalities and justice. In Concha Roldán, Daniel Brauer, and Johannes Rohbeck (eds.) *Philosophy of globalization,* 123–136. Berlin and Boston: Walter de Gruyter. https://doi.org/10. 1515/9783110492415

Dörnyei, Zoltán and Ushioda, Ema. 2011. *Teaching and researching motivation.* Harlow: Pearson Education. https://doi.org/10.4324/9781351006743

Elliot, Anthony, and Charles Lamert. 2010. *The new individualism; The emotional costs of globalisation,* 2nd ed. Oxon: Routledge.

Estellés, Marta, and Gustavo Fischman. 2020. Who needs global citizenship education? A review of the literature on teacher education. *Journal of Teacher Education* 72 (2): 1–14. https://doi.org/10.1177/0022487120920254.

Feng, Mark Teng, and Lixun Wang. 2020. *Identity, motivation, and multilingual education in Asian contexts.* London: Bloomsbury Academic. https://doi.org/10.5040/9781350099685.

Freire, Paulo. 1970. *The pedagogy of the oppressed.* Translated by Myra Bergman Ramos. New York and London: Continuum.

Galloway, Nicola, and Heath Rose. 2015. *Introducing Global Englishes.* London and New York: Routledge. https://doi.org/10.4324/9781315734347.

Gee, James Paul. 2003. *Social linguistics and literacies. Ideology in discourse.* New York: Routledge Falmer. https://doi.org/10.4324/9781315722511

Giddens, Anthony. 2006. Modernity and self-identity: Tribulations of the self. In *The discourse reader*, ed. Adam Jaworski and Nikolas Coupland, 415–427. London: Routledge.

Golding, David. 2017. Border cosmopolitanism in critical peace education. *Journal of Peace Education* 14 (2): 155–175. https://doi.org/10.1080/174 00201.2017.1323727.

Gray, John. 2002. The global coursebook in English language teaching. In David Block and Deborah Cameron (eds.) *Globalization and language teaching*, 105–115. London: Routledge. https://doi.org/10.4324/9780203193679

Hansen, David T. 2008. Curriculum and the idea of a cosmopolitan inheritance. *Journal of Curriculum Studies* 40 (3): 289–312. https://doi.org/10.1080/00220270802036643.

Hasanen, Mohammed M., Al-Kandari, Ali A., and Al Sharoufi, Hussain. 2014. The role of English language and international media as agents of cultural globalisation and their impact on identity formation in Kuwait. *Globalisation, Societies and Education* 12 (4): 542–563. https://doi.org/10.1080/14767724.2013.861972

Henry, Alastair, and Angela Goddard. 2015. Bicultural or hybrid? The second language identities of students on an English-mediated university program in Sweden. *Journal of Language, Identity and Education* 14 (4): 255–274. https://doi.org/10.1080/15348458.2015.1070596.

Hirano, Eliana. 2009. Learning difficulty and learner identity: A symbiotic relationship. *ELT Journal* 63 (1): 33–41. https://doi.org/10.10093/elt/cnn021

Ho, Ya-Yu Cloudia. 2020. Communicative language teaching and English as a foreign language undergraduates' communicative competence in Tourism English. *Journal of Hospitality, Leisure, Sport and Tourism Education* 27: 100271. https://doi.org/10.1016/j.jhlste.2020.100271.

Illés, Éva. 2012. Learner autonomy revisited. *ELT Journal* 66 (4): 505–513. https://doi.org/10.1093/elt/ccs044.

Ivanič, Roz. 1998. *Writing and identity: The discoursal construction of identity in academic writing*. Amsterdam and Philadelphia: John Benjamins.

Jacobson, David. 2001. The global political culture. In *Identities, border, orders: Rethinking international relations theory*, ed. Mathias Albert, David Jacobson, and Yosef Lapid, 161–181. Minneapolis: University of Minnesota.

Jakubiak, Cori. 2020. "English is out there—you have to get with the program": Linguistic instrumentalism, global citizenship education, and English-language voluntourism. *Anthropology and Education* 51 (2): 212–232. https://doi.org/10.1111/aeq.12332.

Jones, Karis M., and Sarah W. Beck. 2020. 'It sound like a paragraph to me': The negotiation of writer identity in dialogic writing assessment. *Linguistics and Education* 55: 100759. https://doi.org/10.1016/j.linged.2019.100759.

Kachru, Braj B. 1985. Standards, codification and sociolinguistic realism: The English language in the outer circle. In Randolph Quirk and Henry George Widdowson (eds.) *English in the World*, 11–32. London: Longman.

Kaldor, Mary. 2003. *Global civil society: An answer to war*. Cambridge: Polity.

Kant, Immanuel. 1957. *Perpetual peace*. Edited by Lewis White Beck. Englewood Cliffs: Macmillan.

Kant, Immanuel. 1978. *Critique of practical reason*. Translated by Lewis White Beck. Indianapolis: Bobbs-Merrill.

Kant, Immanuel. 2002. *Groundwork of the metaphysics of morals*. Translated by Allen W. Wood. New Haven: Yale University Press.

Kant, Immanuel. 2007. Idea for a universal history with a cosmopolitan aim. In *Anthropology, history, and education*, ed. Günter. Zöller and Robert B. Louden, 107–120. Cambridge: Cambridge University Press.

Ke, I-Chung. 2016. Deficient non-native speakers or translanguagers? Identity struggles in a multilingual multimodal ELF online intercultural exchange. *Journal of Asian Pacific Communication* 26(2): 280–300. https://doi.org/10.1075/japc.26.2.06ke

Kleingeld, Pauline. 1998. Kant's cosmopolitan law: World citizenship for a global order. *Kantian Review* 2: 72–90. https://doi.org/10.1017/S136941540000200.

Kleingeld, Pauline. 2012. *Kant and cosmopolitanism: The philosophical ideal of world citizenship*. Cambridge: Cambridge University Press. https://doi.org/10.1017/CBO9781139015486.

Lazos, Efraín. 2018. Hospitality, coercion and peace in Kant. In Concha Roldán, Daniel Brauer, and Johannes Rohbeck (eds.) *Philosophy of globalization*, 327–343. Berlin and Boston: Walter de Gruyter. https://doi.org/10.1515/9783110492415

Liakhovska, Yuliia. 2021. The role of civil society in the formation of civil culture of the future foreign language teacher. *International Journal of Innovative Technologies in Social Science*. https://doi.org/10.31435/rsglobal_ijitss/30092021/7669

Liang, Morita. 2015. English, language shift and values shift in Japan and Singapore. *Globalisation, Societies and Education* 13 (4): 508–527. https://doi.org/10.1080/14767724.2014.967184.

Little, David. 2007. Language learner autonomy: Some fundamental considerations revisited. *Innovation in Language Learning and Teaching* 1 (1): 14–29. https://doi.org/10.2167/illt040.0.

Mallinson, William. 2021. *Guicciardini, geopolitics and geohistory: Understanding inter-state relations*. Cham: Palgrave Macmillan. https://doi.org/10.1007/978-3-030-76537-8_7.

McNamara, Tim. 2019. *Language and subjectivity*. Cambridge: Cambridge University Press. https://doi.org/10.1017/9781108639606.

Mignolo, Walter D. 2000. The many faces of cosmo-polis: Border thinking and critical cosmopolitanism. *Popular Culture* 12 (3): 721–748. https://doi.org/10.1515/9780822383383-007.

Morgan, Brian. 1997. Identity and intonation: Linking dynamic processes in an ESL classroom. *TESOL Quarterly* 31 (3): 431–450. https://doi.org/10.2307/3587833.

Norton, Bonny. 2001. Non-participation, imagined communities and the language classroom. In *Learner contributions to language learning*, ed. Michael P. Breen, 159–171. Harlow: Longman.

Norton, Bonny and Pavlenko, Aneta. 2019. Imagined communities, identity, and English language learning in a multilingual world. In Xuesong Gao (ed.) *Second handbook of English language teaching*, 703–718. Switzerland AG: Springer Nature. https://doi.org/10.1007/978-3-030-02899-2_34

Patel, Fay, and Hayley Lynch. 2013. Glocalization as an alternative to internationalization in higher education: Embedding positive glocal learning perspectives. *International Journal of Teaching and Learning in Higher Education* 25 (2): 223–230.

Pennycook, Alastair. 1997. Cultural alternatives and autonomy. In Phil Benson and Peter Voller (eds.) *Autonomy and independence in language learning*, 35–53. London: Longman. https://doi.org/10.4324/9781315842172-4

Pieterse, Jan Nedervee. 1995. Globalization as hybridization. In Mike Featherstone, Scott Lash, and Roland Robertson (eds.) *Global modernities*, 45–68. London: Sage. https://doi.org/10.4135/9781446250563

Pineda, Inmaculada, Wenli Tsou, and Fay Chen. 2022. Glocalization in CLIL: Analyzing the training needs of in-service CLIL teachers in Taiwan and Spain. *Journal of Multilingual and Multicultural Development*. https://doi.org/10.1080/01434632.2022.2050380.

Richards, Jack C. 2021. Teacher, learner and student–teacher identity in TESOL. *RELC Journal* 54 (1): 252–266. https://doi.org/10.1177/003368822199 1308.

Richards, Keith. 2006. 'Being the teacher': Identity and classroom conversation. *Applied Linguistics* 27 (1): 51–77. https://doi.org/10.1093/applin/ami041.

Risager, Karen. 2018. *Representations of the world in language textbooks*. Bristol: Multilingual Matters. https://doi.org/10.21832/9781783099566

Robertson, Roland. 1995. *Globalization: Social theory and global culture*. London: Sage. https://doi.org/10.4135/9781446280447.

Rohbeck, Johannes. 2018. Global responsibility in a historical context. In Concha Roldán, Daniel Brauer, and Johannes Rohbeck (eds.) *Philosophy of globalization*, 179–188. Berlin and Boston: Walter de Gruyter. https://doi.org/10.1515/9783110492415

Rose, Heath, and Nicola Galloway. 2019. *Global Englishes for language teaching*. Cambridge: Cambridge University Press. https://doi.org/10.1017/978131 6678343.

Roudometof, Victor. 2016. *Glocalization: A critical introduction*. London and New York: Routledge. https://doi.org/10.4324/9781315858296.

Salih, Abdelrahman A., and Lamis I. Omar. 2021. Globalized English and users' intercultural awareness: Implications for internationalization of higher education. *Citizenship, Social and Economics Education* 20 (3): 181–196. https://doi.org/10.1177/20471734211037660.

Sert, Sibel, and Yonca Özkan. 2020. Implementing ELF-informed activities in an elementary level English preparatory classroom. *Multicultural Learning and Teaching* 15 (1): 1–15. https://doi.org/10.1515/mlt-2018-0003.

Shani, Giorgio. 2003. 'The liberal project': Globalization, modernity and identity. *Ritsumeikan Annual Review of International Studies* 2: 37–57.

Shin, Jeeyoung, Zohreh Rasekh Eslami, and Wen-Chun. Chen. 2011. Presentation of local and international culture in current international English-language teaching textbook. *Language, Culture and Curriculum* 24 (3): 253–268. https://doi.org/10.1080/07908318.2011.614694.

Sifakis, Nicos C. 2014. ELF awareness as an opportunity for change: A transformative perspective for ESOL teacher education. *Journal of English as a Lingua Franca* 3 (2): 317–335. https://doi.org/10.1515/jelf-2014-0019.

Song, Heejin. 2013. Deconstruction of cultural dominance in Korean EFL textbooks. *Intercultural Education* 24 (4): 382–390. https://doi.org/10.1080/14675986.2013.809248.

Soruç, Adem, and Carol Griffiths. 2015. Identity and the spoken grammar dilemma. *System* 50: 32–42. https://doi.org/10.1016/j.system.2015.03.007.

Sun, Xiaoan. 2020. Towards a common framework for global citizenship education: A critical review of UNESCO's conceptual framework of global citizenship education. In Xudong Zhu, Jiayong Li, Mang Li, Qiang Liu, and Hugh Starkey (eds.) *Education and mobilities, perspectives on rethinking and reforming education*, 263–277. Singapore: Springer Nature. https://doi.org/10.1007/978-981-13-9031-9_15

Sun, Tingting, and Adcharawan Buripakdi. 2023. Unpacking Chinese primary school English teachers' perceptions: Personal blockers and enablers in global citizenship education. *Asia Pacific Journal of Education*. https://doi.org/10.1080/02188791.2023.2235918.

Sung, Chit Cheung Matthew. 2014. English as a lingua franca and global identities: Perspectives from four second language learners of English in Hong Kong. *Linguistics and Education* 26: 31–39. https://doi.org/10.1016/j.linged.2014.01.010

Syrbe, Mona, and Heath Rose. 2018. An evaluation of the global orientation of English textbooks in Germany. *Innovation in Language Learning and Teaching* 12 (2): 152–163. https://doi.org/10.1080/17501229.2015.1120736.

Tarozzi, Massimiliano, and Torrres, Carlos Alberto. 2016. *Global citizenship education and the crises of multiculturalism: Comparative perspectives*. London and New York: Bloomsbury Academic. https://doi.org/10.5040/9781474236003

Wang, Ying 2020. The role of English in higher education internationalization: Language ideologies on EMI programmes in China. In Hugo Bowles and Amanda C. Murphy (eds.) *English-medium instruction and the internationalization of universities*, 103–128. Cham: Palgrave Macmillan. https://doi.org/10.1007/978-3-030-47860-5

Wu, Manfred Man-fat. 2016. Implications of Hegel's theories of language on second language teaching. *Journal of Curriculum Studies* 48 (3): 346–366. https://doi.org/10.1080/00220272.2016.1151081.

Wu, Manfred Man-fat. 2020. Second language teaching for global citizenship. *Globalisation, Societies and Education* 18 (3): 330–342. https://doi.org/10.1080/14767724.2019.1693349.

Wu, Manfred Man-fat, Römhild, Ricardo, and Nishizaki, Mona. In press. Teaching English as an international language for global citizenship. In Nicola Galloway and Ali Fuad Selvi (eds.) *The Routledge handbook of English as an international language*. Routledge.

Xu, Zhichang. 2013. Globalization, culture and ELT materials: A focus on China. *Multilingual Education* 3 (6). https://doi.org/10.1186/2191-5059-3-6

Zajda, Joseph, and Val Rust. 2021. *Globalisation and comparative education*. Dordrecht: Springer. https://doi.org/10.1007/978-94-024-2054-8_11.

Zhang, Chunyan and Semple, Cheryl. 2016. The emotional costs of a globalising learner identity: Challenges and opportunities for 21st century pedagogy in the Asian century. In Tasos Barkatsas and Adam Bertram (eds.) *Global learning in the 21st century*, 213–230. Rotterdam: Sense Publishers. https://doi.org/10.1007/978-94-6300-761-0

Zhang, Yan, and Yan Guo. 2015. Becoming transnational: Exploring multiple identities of students in a Mandarin-English bilingual programme in Canada. *Globalisation, Societies and Education* 13 (2): 210–229. https://doi.org/10.1080/14767724.2014.934071.

Zhang, Zhe (Victor). 2022. Identity construction and second language acquisition: A multiple case study of Thai immigrants in Hong Kong. *Journal of Language Identity & Education.* https://doi.org/10.1080/15348458.2021.1999816

Zimmerman, Don H. 1998. Discoursal identities and social identities. In *Identities in talk*, ed. Charles Antaki and Sue Widdicombe, 87–106. London: Sage.

CHAPTER 3

Dilemmas of L2 Identity in Globalisation and the Hegelian Solution of Morality

Abstract This chapter discusses four dilemmas of L2 identity in the context of globalisation raised by Giddens (*The discourse reader*. Routledge, London, 2006). According to Giddens (2006), globalisation has exerted a force for unification with other parts of the world for self-identity while simultaneously raising concerns for self-preservation. Secondly, individuals feel powerless in the globalised context due to a lack of control. However, globalisation has posed new opportunities and resources for individuals to appropriate and re-appropriate resources for their life circumstances. Thirdly, globalisation has resulted in the demise of authority and religion and resulted in uncertainties caused by a plurality of authorities. Finally, commodification has resulted in personalised consumption made up of standardised products, which causes pathological over-individualisation of consumption. Hegel emphasises pure duty, and more importantly, its actualisation in his anthro-political philosophy. Hegelian morality is proposed to empower individuals in resolving the tensions in these four dilemmas. This is achieved by using English as a lingua franca in interacting with others from different parts of the globe and inculcating a globalised L2 identity.

Keywords Anthony Giddens · Dilemmas · Globalisation · L2 identity · Hegel · Pure duty · Morality

© The Author(s), under exclusive license to Springer Nature Switzerland AG 2024
M. M. Wu, *Globalisation and Second Language Identity*,
https://doi.org/10.1007/978-3-031-68248-3_3

49

INTRODUCTION

Economic and cultural globalisation, ethnocentric nationalism and global risks have been offered as the reasons for a resurgence of research interest in global citizenship (see Cavallar 2014). Giddens poses four dilemmas of self in the contemporary age of globalisation. According to him, although there seems to be little difference in contemporary society as most of us are living a local life, in fact, the "phenomenal worlds for the most part are truly global" (Giddens 2006: 415).

Giddens's four dilemmas of self in the context of globalisation are highly pertinent as an analytical framework for analysing how globalisation exerts influences on L2 identity. This chapter discusses the dilemmas faced by L2 learners in the context of globalisation, and offers support for the view that Giddens's dilemmas are equally applicable to L2 learners. It also highlights the lack of consideration of morality in research and discussions on L2 identity of learners in the context of globalisation, a major theme of this book. Finally, this chapter proposes the infusion of morality from the Hegelian perspective, which focuses on taking action to fulfill one's duties to others, as a solution to Giddens's dilemmas.

Details of Giddens's dilemmas are introduced below.

DILEMMAS OF SELF IN GLOBALISATION

Dilemma 1: Unification Versus Fragmentation

Giddens's first dilemma is Unification versus Fragmentation, which means that increasing globalisation has exerted a force for unification with other parts of the world for self-identity, while simultaneously raising concerns for the preservation of self in facing the mass external changes. With powerful communication technology and mass media, distant events may become prominent ones. Thus, contemporary self-identity may be established by elements from diversified contexts that are fragmentary in nature, and "a cosmopolitan person is one precisely who draws strengths from being at home in a variety of contexts" (Giddens 2006: 418). Countries such as South Korea (Song 2013) and Japan (Liang 2015; Saito 2018) have been struggling with whether to adopt English as a medium of instruction in schools in facing the challenges globalisation has brought for fear that their national identity will be undermined. Initiatives such as the indigenous-language immersion programme advocated by McCarty et al. (2021)[1] can be regarded as an attempt at the preservation of heritage self. Gholami (2017) calls for a more sophisticated understanding of how identity is formed and performed for the promotion of global citizenship in the UK influenced by the increasing extent of globalisation.

Dilemma 2: Powerlessness Versus Appropriation

The second dilemma is Powerlessness versus Appropriation. Contrary to the common view that individuals in pre-modern society are more powerless because of traditions, Giddens (2006) explains that individuals are more powerless in the modern globalised society because the control of influences shaping life has passed to multiple external agencies such as multinational corporations and supranational organisations like the World Trade Organization. The time–space distanciation (the disconnection between time and space) caused by technology and the de-skilling effects due to automation also contribute to the powerlessness of individuals.

Despite bringing about powerlessness, globalisation has made available many unprecedented possibilities for individuals to appropriate and re-appropriate resources, such as the low cost of communication and consumer product delivery, and geographical mobility thanks to advanced transportation systems, for their life circumstances. These resources significantly altered the choices of lifestyle, including ways of L2 learning for individuals. An example is that before the prevalence of the Internet learners had limited public resources for L2 learning, at present they are faced with too much (Benson and Lamb 2020). The lack of knowledge and skills for choosing suitable resources may create a sense of powerlessness among them. Through exercising a sense of duty to others, for example, making conscientious suggestions to fellow learners on the websites for L2 learning and online programmes to enroll, individuals develop their positive L2 identity and empower their fellow learners.

Dilemma 3: Authority Versus Uncertainty

The third dilemma, Authority versus Uncertainty, refers to the demise of tradition and religion (which prescribe moral principles for behaviours)

---

[1] This proposal by McCarty et al. (2021) has a strong cultural base. It emphasises promoting language revitalisation, cultural identity and continuance, and sustainability.

as the authority, with the authority replaced by plurality of authorities or agencies. The plurality of authorities may give rise to the feeling of uncertainty for globalised individuals because of the very often contradictory demands exerted by different agencies such as the globalised market, financial system, public services, education, law and order, security, and international organisations.[2]

In globalised societies, individuals live in uncertainties because of the increasing number of influences that are outside their control. Gholami (2017) argues that "young people's assertions of identity are often (re)performances of ideas and ideals of selfhood which have been shaped by highly discontinuous, even contradictory, social, cultural and political realities across multiple times and spaces" (806). To overcome the institutional globalisation "from above", Torres (2012; see also Tarozzi and Torres 2016) recommends globalisation "from below", which involves cosmopolitan globalisation of human rights.[3] Despite the uncertainties, Giddens contends that rationalisation of social institutions has established routines and makes life more predictable.[4] However, individuals face psychological pressure because of the existence of diverse and mutually conflicting authorities.

Dilemma 4: Personalised Versus Commercial Experience

The last dilemma is Personalised versus Commercial Experience. Commodification and consumption have become a key ingredient in the process of self-identity devleopment in the globalised world. Self-actualisation in modern society is achieved through the possession of standardised goods promoted based on market criteria. Despite designing consumptions based on personalised needs and wants, what the capitalist market offers is actually standardised in nature. This over-individuation of consumption, according to Giddens (2006), may cause pathologies such as narcissism and grandiosity, which adversely affect the construction of a healthy self-identity. Elliot and Lamert (2010) offer an account of the

---

[2] For example, Torres (2012) criticises privatisation, culture of measure, science as power and fetishism of technology resulted from globalisation.

[3] Torres (2012) remarks that the globalisation of human rights sometimes are in tension with national policies. See also Wu (2020).

[4] For example, schedules of public transportations have become more accurate and information on possible natural disasters has become more readily available.

emotional cost individuals need to pay for globalisation. According to them, globalisation has resulted in a new form of individualism that is characterised by a craze for continuous re-definition of self and endless hunger for instant change. These trends exert negative influences on the emotions of individuals.

The commodification of language has also given rise to the exponential increase in the standardised commercial L2 learning packages ubiquitously available in the electronic markets, which again exerts profound influences on the L2 identity of learners. An example is the large number of online L2 learning courses available in the market mostly provided by native speakers which may give the impression among learners that a native accent is the target for their L2 learning. The uncensored provision of language courses may also create conflicting perceptions of the competence required for successful L2 learning. This alienating feature of the globalised world poses difficulties for the successful achievement of mutual recognition, a key element of self-identity construction and social bonding in Hegel's (1971; 1977; see also Wu 2016) anthro-political philosophy. The interpersonal exchanges based on material possession promoted by the mass media result in incomplete recognition.

Language, Morality, and Globalisation

Despite not having the intention to relate globalisation and self-identity with morality, the above account by Giddens indicates the need for morality in resolving the four dilemmas. The first dilemma has resulted in a need for preservation of self. As will be explained in detail below, from a Hegelian perspective morality, or more specifically, conscience, is an integral part of consciousness and thus self-identity. Moral consciousness gains its content in language and achieves reality, and language makes conscience's beliefs valid.[5] The second and third dilemmas describe that individuals are powerless in the globalised world and are facing uncertainty with the diminishing influence of religion (including morality) and a growing plurality of authorities. Pennycook (2021) laments the lack of attention given to ethics and the need for an ethical vision in the field

---

[5] As stated by Liu et al. (2021), "[I]n 'Morality', language is what brings reality and existence to self-consciousness. Language has the ability to make self-consciousness real ... Conscience is just moral consciousness that gains its content in language, thus achieving reality." (11)

of applied linguistics. Morality, in the Hegelian sense the actualisation of one's duties to others through taking actions, empowers individuals with ethical prowess and facilitates the resolution of these dilemmas. Finally, the pathologies caused by standardised goods for consumption in the globalised world can be ameliorated by strengthening the moral prowess and autonomy in the moral sense (Kant 2002) of individuals such as increasing self-awareness and being informed of ways to resist the temptation of excessive and pathological consumption. Globalisation involves power struggles that can be coercive or collaborative.[6] Morality can equip L2 learners to make proper judgements and to take actions in facing the challenges posed by globalisation.

Language is the integral constituent of self and identity, and is therefore intimately related to the above dilemmas. The recent trend of "linguistic turns" in philosophy shows a greater awareness of the role of language both in philosophy and identity.[7] A major aim of this chapter is to discuss how the Hegelian perspective can offer solutions to resolve the dilemmas raised by Giddens, which is equally applicable to research and discussions on L2 identity.

Although Hegel did not explain how language functions in international relations and globalisation, his discussions on how language enables the Spirit, the collective human consciousness, or the impersonal logical concept,[8] to manifest itself in the objective reality indicate that the role of language is indispensable in international affairs. Hegel's (2008) *Philosophy of right* is devoted to elicitations of how Spirit unfolds itself to the objective reality, in the realms of family, civil society, corporation, state, legislature, international relations, and world history. These realms have determining influences on the development of self-identity for individuals. In these descriptions, Hegel makes references to how language enables the unfolding process to occur and complete with the ultimate goal of creating a harmonious global collective human entity.

In international relations, a common language is very often used for contracts and agreements in trade, national borders, defence, national security, immigration, and other policies. Hegel concurs with Kant (1957,

---

[6] According to Cummins (1996), coercive relations refer to a dominant individual, group or country exercising power to maintain an unequal power relationship in a society. Collaborative power relations, on the other hand, are empowering.

[7] For example, Losonsky (2006).

[8] See Wu (2023).

2002) in viewing that compared to state law which is universal and obligatory, international law depends on the constraining power of the state (Hegel 1953). This implies that a common language, very often English, has a vital role in both the preparation and successful implementation and maintenance of international order. The significance of English as a lingua franca at the international level inevitably exerts influences on the L2 identity of learners, for example, on attributing values of L2 in terms of access to information, entertainment, and career development.

As pointed out in Chapter 1, language is intimately linked to morality. For example, language can motivate individuals to act in ways prescribed by morality rules (Curry et al. 2019) and language represents the morality of a community. As L2 identity determines how one perceives himself in L2 learning, it exerts influences on not only their own learning but also their views on those using English as a common language and their behaviours in their exchange with them. At the same time, exerting positive influences on L2 identity can alter individuals' beliefs and behaviours, which can enable them to thrive in the globalisation context.

In the next section, a brief review of the literature on L2 identity and globalisation to date, with particular reference to Giddens's four dilemmas of self, will be summarised. This is followed by discussions on how the Hegelian notion of morality can contribute to resolving the dilemmas.

Recent Post-structural Research on L2 Identity

Recent research on L2 identity has been nuanced with the post-structural approaches centring on power, ideology, and fluidity of L2 identity. De Costa (2016a) describes the powerful influences of ideology in an age of globalisation on L2 identity. He conducted an ethnographic research study of five immigrant Grade 9 (Secondary 3) students in Singapore, who he termed designer immigrant students because they were attracted by the foreign talent scheme of the Singapore government. His research explored how the school became "a site for struggle for these designer immigrant students as they wrestle with a hegemonic language ideology and a cosmopolitan identity that demanded homogeneity by way of English language standardization" (De Costa 2016a: 1). De Costa (2016a) identified a "designer immigrant complex" among these elite students, that they were marginalised despite being high academic achievers, and were under the conflictual forces of the official use of standard English and the unofficial use of Singlish.

Norton discusses how the changing conceptualisations of the individual, language, and learning influence the theoretical development and research on L2 identity (Norton 2013). According to her, the recent post-structural turn has changed the view of individual from having fixed traits to that of diverse, contradictory, and dynamic. This results in discussions on personal identity in relation to power and inequality. The post-structural view also treats language as an ideological tool for struggle, and linguistic communities are heterogeneous containing conflicting claims to truth and power, which inevitably results in the emergence of winners and losers, thus a sense of powerlessness. Finally, the social constructivist approach represented by Vygotsky (1986, 1987) treats learning as a social endeavour. Similar to Hegel, Vygotsky views that individuals and society are in continuous tension, and these forces contribute to the emergence of alternative conceptualisations on L2 identity and new lines of research. L2 identity is constantly changing as

> [e]very time language learners interact in the second language, whether in the oral or written mode, they are engaged in identity construction and negotiation (Norton 2013: 3).

The post-structural view on L2 identity converges with Giddens's observation on the fragmentary nature of identity and the powerlessness experienced by the individual and the uncertainty caused by demising influences of religion (in which morality is a significant constituent) in the globalised world. Despite their convergence, they both fail to offer solutions and neglect the significance of morality in overcoming the challenges. Results of the empirical research undertaken by Rutgers et al. (2024) provide evidence of the need to examine the attitudinal and emotional aspects of identity. They found that students' self-ascribed multilingual identity, compared to school-ascribed multilingual identity, has stronger positive correlations with academic attainments. Moreover, it is able to predict the performance of more academic subjects. This means that the cognitive aspect compared to the attitudinal aspect of multilingual identity has only limited explanatory power in accounting for the academic performance of students.

Globalisation caused the commodification of language and therefore the use of standardised English is vital to the economic development of a country. The designer immigrant students in De Costa's (2016a) study were regarded as superior in terms of academic performance at the same time were endowed with linguistic repertoires of their native countries. Facing unequal power between them and the education system, they were marginalised despite their outstanding academic performance. This, as proposed by De Costa, created a designer immigrant student complex that negatively affected the language acquisition experience, and inevitably L2 identity development, of these learners.

De Costa's (2016a) solution to the complex is a reconceptualisation of language along ideological, semiotic, and performative lines. His description is related to the dilemma of Unification vs Fragmentation raised by Giddens and indicates the fragmentation effects of globalisation. The marginalisation experienced by the designer immigrant students also caused a sense of powerlessness as a result of globalisation. Although in the above example, the uncertainty was not caused by the demising influence of religion, it is ideological in nature. As will be further explained in the next section, morality in the Hegelian sense is a promising solution for remedying this marginalisation phenomenon caused by globalisation.

Lo-Philip and Park (2015) adopt a discoursal approach to analyse the tensions in L2 identity. They gathered empirical data from three students at a bilingual Mandarin Chinese English secondary school in Singapore, and explored their individual differences by examining how their unique sets of discourses and everyday lived experiences contributed to the construction of their L2 identity. Their research was based on the notion of dialogic imagining, or how individuals make sense of their bilingual experiences in interacting with others. They labelled the three selves of the participants as subverting race, flexible self, and blending to other cultures, and each of them shows the uniqueness of their L2 identity make-up. This multi-dimensional nature of L2 identity shows the influences of powerlessness in Giddens's second dilemma and the plurality of agencies in his third dilemma. Although Lo-Philip and Park (2015) vividly demonstrated how discourses shape globalised identity, again, no consideration on morality was made in their research. Their recommendations are that in fostering a flexible L2 identity, students need to be encouraged to reflect on their bilingual experiences, be informed about how language is related to culture, race, and identity, and students should "hear, share, challenge, and struggle with different perspectives than their own" (203). In short, they recommend the enhancement of the language, cultural, and identity awareness of students.

As described in the first dilemma, the tensions between globalisation and national identity have led countries, especially Southeast Asian countries (see Fitriati and Rata 2021) to re-consider their national language policies. This phenomenon is related to Giddens's (2006) first dilemma. In addition to the situations of Korea and Japan introduced in relation to the first dilemma, in Indonesia, Fitriati and Rata (2021) report teachers' attitudes, reluctance, and difficulties in implementing English medium instruction to academic subjects in schools have led the state to withdraw the policy and revert to using Indonesian for teaching. This is despite the state's intention to be recognised as an international member of the global economy. According to Fitriati and Rata (2021), these tensions were also caused by the active promotion of nation state of cultural homogenisation for its members.

The above phenomenon echoes the observation given by Harris et al. (2002) on the tensions posed to the linguistically diverse group among ethnic minorities in inner London at the expense of unification with the national language landscape. Gao et al. (2015) also documented the complexity and ambivalence of L2 identity among learners in the context of globalisation in China, which again is a manifestation of the tensions involved in Giddens's first dilemma of Unification vs Fragmentation. After experiencing a drop in their linguistic self-confidence in their first year of study, undergraduates in China developed their sense of competence in the remaining years of their university studies. More importantly, their first language identity and culture were found to be replaced by that of English, and tensions were identified in the process.

Multiple language identity membership affects an individual's reactions to Giddens's (2006) dilemmas of self in the context of globalisation. This is because with more memberships an individual will be more likely to feel socially unified instead of isolated. At the same time, multiple and a well-balanced multiple language identity empowers an individual in overcoming the powerlessness caused by globalisation, and enables them to locate appropriate resources made available by globalisation. However, multiple identity membership may at the same time result in uncertainties because of the plurality of authorities. Finally, multiple language identity membership harnesses individuals with resources such as the latest information for making decisions on their consumption and the capacity to notice the caveats caused by over-commodification and over-consumption. Multiple language identity needs to work together with morality in order for individuals to maintain their healthy L2 identity.

The conflicts that exist in L2 identity in the globalised context resonate with the Hegelian (e.g., 1977) view of the self as a site for struggle and the dialectical process involved, as it was found that L2 identity development does not follow a linear pattern (e.g., Gao et al. 2015). In addition to De Costa (2016a) described above, Lu (2020) recounts the import of academically elite students in Singapore of Chinese ethnicity from China and Vietnam did not result in the successful integration of these elite students into Singaporean schools. In the Turkish context, Tulgar (2021) identified an increasing awareness of local identities, adaptation of them to their global identity, and the formation of a glocal identity among international students who participated in her study. Again, the development of L2 identity was found to involve uncertainties, tensions, negotiation, and renegotiation of meanings and again being non-linear (i.e., dialectical) in nature, indicating Giddens's fragmentation of self and powerlessness of individuals in facing globalisation. Harnessing learners with morality prowess, especially in the Hegelian action-oriented sense (see, for example, Rockmore 1997), is a good way to resolve dilemmas. A common view that prevails among applied linguists is that identities are constructed in social action (see De Costa 2016b).

Taken as a whole, research on L2 identity and globalisation has largely been adopted an integrative, assimilative, and cognitive perspectives, and insufficient attention has been given to powerlessness, uncertainty, personalisation, and commercialisation raised by Giddens, not to mention morality. However, the above summary provides support for the dilemmas, which means that Giddens's dilemmas exist for L2 identity in the globalised context. There have been calls for research on the notion of an ideal global language identity (see Gao et al. 2015) which may embrace morality, but so far this topic has been relatively neglected. To reiterate, morality in the Hegelian sense, which is taking action to realise pure duty, is suggested in this book as a viable means to resolve the tensions caused by globalisation for L2 learners. The details are introduced in the next section.

HEGELIAN MORALITY AS THE SOLUTION FOR DILEMMAS OF SELF IN GLOBALISATION

Hegel's philosophical perspective is anthro-political in nature. The main thesis of his philosophy is that the collective human consciousness evolves or progresses in a developmental manner, from mere awareness of their surroundings through the senses to awareness of self and others, and finally reaches Absolute Knowledge, or "knowledge that is unbiased, undistorted, unqualified, all-encompassing, free from counter-examples and internal inconsistencies. Opposed to: relative, qualified, conditioned, abstract, partial.... It means having an adequate conception of knowledge and the Absolute, and understanding that there is no separation or 'epistemological gap' between them" (Solomon 1983: 274). Of particular relevance to the focus of this book is Hegel's emphasis on the others, which enables mutual recognition and intersubjectivity to occur through a dialectical process (Wu 2016). According to Hegel (1971, 1977), in encountering an "other", an individual (consciousness) experiences negation or alienation, loses himself, and after being recognised by the other, he gains a sense of self and becomes more self-conscious. This process is achieved through a dialectical process, which Hegel used extensively throughout his works and is accounted for in his *Science of Logic* (Hegel 1969), involving positedness, negation, and sublation to result in higher and more abstract stages of development. These processes, both intrapersonally and interpersonally, involve the use of language.

Unlike Kant (1957, 1978, 2002) who mainly focused on pure duty, Hegel focuses on acting out pure duty as the key feature of morality (Hegel 1977). According to him, there are contradictions between morality or conscience and reality, and these contradictions give rise to struggles for the collective human consciousness to progress to Absolute Knowing. It is only by combining pure duty with actuality that morality can be actualised. Another feature of Hegelian morality is that the action must be exerted on another being, and as stated by Hegel, "(P)ure duty has also in point of fact validity only in another being, not in the morality consciousness" (Hegel 1977: 380).

Under the backdrop of the importance of others, intersubjectivity, dialectic, and pure duty and its actualisation, how Hegelian morality can potentially resolve the four dilemmas Giddens will be explored in the remainder of this section.

Dilemma 1: Unification Versus Fragmentation

In Europe, linguistic minorities are searching for their cultural identity under the multilingual context, and this enables them to discover or rediscover their own identity (Marga 2010). This on the surface seems to cause fragmentation as suggested by Giddens (2006). However, at the same time, this has led to a call for education for democratic citizenship and equal dignity (see Marga 2010), which are moral in nature. There has been an awareness of the following issues in Europe: the dangers of unrestrained and unlimited autonomy of ethnic minorities of the laissez-faire attitudes; the homogenisation of nation state; a need for the cultivation of tolerance in the modern states on individualism; and the recognition of collective rights "without curtailing individualistic structure of legislation" (Marga 2010: 52). The final two elements are moral in nature, and these issues concur with Giddens's first three dilemmas. Marga's (2010) arguments and evidence suggest that unification in terms of cultural and ethnic identity (and therefore morality) instead of fragmentation predominates or is at least encouraged in multilingual Europe.

According to Ivanič (1998), although Halliday (1994) describes how language contributes to identity through conveying "interpersonal meaning", he did not pay enough attention to it. Ivanič (1998) devises three components that correspond to the above three functions and adopted them as the theoretical framework of his study. The first component is a person's set of values and beliefs about reality, which correspond to Halliday's "ideational meaning". The second component is a person's sense of their relative status in relation to others, which affects Halliday's "interpersonal meaning". The third component is a person's orientation on language use, which influences the way they construct their message. As far as intertextual approaches are concerned, Ivanič (1998) adopts interdiscursivity as a key component of his framework. Interdiscursivity is a powerful concept because it explains how people make their discoursal choices that are available to them and is able to connect their past and future. Findings of his interviews with adult learners provide evidence that individuals are connected to the dominant ideology and are therefore influenced by morality. However, the crucial step of acting out morality proposed by Hegel is missing in the accounts of Ivanič (1998) Halliday (1994).

The discoursal approach can unify instead of resulting in fragmentation. A good example is Lo-Philip and Park (2015), who propose raising learners' awareness of how language and culture complexly shape and influence their L2 identity. However, as stated repeatedly in this chapter, the important Hegelian notion of morality should be infused in fostering globalised L2 identity of learners. The inclusion of morality in the cultivation of L2 identity can enable learners to take multiple perspectives in viewing themselves and others (through infusing a sense of duty to others), which in turn can resolve the sense of isolation, alienation, uncertainties, and fluctuations experienced by learners (Gao et al. 2015; Lu 2020; Tulgar 2021) and countries (e.g., Song 2013).

Dilemma 2: Powerlessness Versus Appropriation

To overcome the feeling of powerlessness, awareness of the pure duty to others and actualising it are essential in the globalised context. This is especially true because of time–space distanciation caused by electronic communication technology (Chayko 2021), which may result in alienation for individuals. The social system, because of the control by multiple agencies caused by globalisation, especially the increasing complexity and differentiation of jobs, tends to deskill individuals and renders skills of individuals obsolete rapidly. Again, facing this uncertainty, individuals need to act according to their conscience (through the use of language) not only to survive in the globalised world and overcome the feeling of powerlessness, but also to change the world positively and collectively. Equally important is that morality can harness learners to make sensible and rational judgements in appropriating and re-appropriating resources brought by globalisation, for example, in choosing language to learn and viewing themselves positively as L2 learners.

Dilemma 3: Authority Versus Uncertainty

As stated earlier, morality is particularly useful for resolving the tensions caused by the demise of tradition and religion, which have been replaced by a fragmentary plurality of authorities. As illustrated by the results of research such as De Costa's (2016a), the influences of ideology on L2 learners have been more and more prevalent due to the increasing extent of globalisation worldwide. More and more discussions and research from the post-structural perspective have revealed the powerlessness and uncertainties L2 learners are experiencing (e.g., Nematzadeh and Narafshan 2020). Compared to the situation in the past, individuals in the contemporary globalised world are free from the constraints of tradition. However, at the same time, they need to be highly autonomous and responsible for their actions (Wu 2023). Without morality, this can hardly be achieved. Facing the plurality of authorities such as the government, education and language policy, economy, legal system which very often seem unrelated and even contradictory, individuals experience difficulty in making sense of their life. Morality, a consistent sense of right and wrong, and acting out conscience can help individuals overcome uncertainties caused by a lack of authority.

Dilemma 4: Personalised Versus Commercial Experience

Riley (2006), who proposes that the notion of ethics contributes to L2 identity, provides empirical evidence for a number of negotiation strategies between service providers and clients which are described below. He gathered video recordings of the interactions between the two parties in the commercial sector and identified three strategies of negotiation for membership: identity affirmation, use of domain-specific discourse, and specific choice of language, among his research participants. According to him, anecdotes are "passages of monologistic narrative of varying length embedded in stretches of interactive discourse" (Riley 2006: 311), and this mechanism found in the interviews was used by individuals for self-expression of shared meanings constructed through interacting with others in constructing their L2 identity. Pragmatic failure, or the misunderstanding caused by the application of inappropriate social rules or knowledge in discoursal and communicative behaviours, is related to negotiation because the competence to avoid pragmatic failure is the essential competence for identity negotiation.

L2 identity is constructed from ethics through the above negotiation strategies. Negotiation is important in individuals' personalised versus commercial experience, because in order to function effectively in the commodified global market, individuals need strong competence in the negotiation of meanings, both face-to-face and through electronic communications. This is because cyberspace is packed with persuasive commercial messages which are often hard to distinguish from objective information. Besides negotiation, individuals' L2 identity in the globalised context is highly related to how they perceive others, especially those they perceive to encounter in the cyberworld. Again, "imagined communities" (Kanno and Norton 2003) exert heavy influences on the L2 identity and behaviours of globalised learners.

Due to globalisation, language is no longer tied to locality, and there are four conditions for the existence of an imagined community: membership, community's influence on members, identity reinforcement by community membership, and shared affective connections (De Costa and Green-Eneix 2021). One view of Ryan (2006) is that given the influences of globalisation, individuals have to "construct their own identity with reference to their 'local manifestation of global values'" (33). This contributes to the fragmentary and dynamic nature of globalised L2 identity and uncertainty caused by a lack of authority caused by globalisation. This is especially true with contemporary nation states being active in the promotion of the cultural homogenisation of its members (see Fitriati and Rata 2021). Again, the above account indicates the need for morality—pure duty and its actualisation through performing actions and exerting influences on reality in the Hegelian sense.

Conclusion

This chapter began by introducing the four dilemmas of self in the context of globalisation raised by Giddens (2006), namely, Unification versus Fragmentation, Powerlessness versus Appropriation, Authority versus Uncertainty, and Personalised versus Commercial Experience. The relevance of these four dilemmas to research, discussions, and teaching on L2 identity was discussed. It was found that the four dilemmas are equally applicable to L2 identity, as indicated by research and discussions in this area.

This chapter has proposed morality from a Hegelian perspective be adopted to resolve the dilemmas of self in the context of globalisation raised by Giddens (2006). More specifically, morality can resolve the first dilemma by bringing together and consolidating the fragmented elements of identity caused by diversified elements in the globalised world. Morality can resolve the second dilemma of feeling powerless by equipping individuals with the moral prowess to face augmented uncertainties both in type and extent caused by increasing control by multiple agencies on individuals' life. Morality can provide a replacement for authority caused by the demise of the influences of religion (which includes morality) and enhance individual autonomy. Finally, morality can complement the lack of mutual recognition caused by commodification and standardisation of products, because morality is able to provide a sense of right and wrong, and enables individuals to feel at home with their conscience.

The social constructivists view classroom learning as a part of reality, as socially constructed from syntheses of subjectivities between teachers and students involving ideologies (De Costa and Green-Eneix2021 Gray and Morton 2018). The Hegelian perspective on recognition also suggests that the identities of teachers and students of their L2 learning are mutually influenced by each other (Wu 2016). Therefore, in the inclusion of moral elements in the nurturing of L2 identity of learners, teachers need to be equipped with Hegelian morality. At present, materials and training on global L2 identity available for teachers are hardly available, not to mention those infused with moral elements. Therefore, in devising strategies for fostering globalised L2 identity, awareness of how personal history influences and can be utilised for L2 identity of learners on the part of the teacher is particularly important.

Given the high compatibility of Hegelian philosophy of language to the historical and contemporary developments on the implementation approaches to fostering L2 identity as demonstrated in this chapter, infusing Hegelian morality into L2 identity research and implementation is a potentially fruitful direction. Recommendations offered in Chapter 2 on overcoming the challenges to L2 identity posed by globalisation are equally effective in resolving Giddens's dilemmas of self discussed in this chapter. Adopting L2 teaching as a means for the cultivation of morality has not yet been popular. Two exceptions are Poon (2010) as well as Porto and Zembylas (2020), with the former expressing that the Singapore English literature syllabus regards literature as a means for students to explore moral and social issues, and the latter using arts and literature to cultivate learner empathy and solidarity. Phan (2008), on the other hand, points out that English teachers are very often regarded as models of social morality. More similar attempts especially on the empirical level should be made to validate the potential use of morality in resolving the dilemmas of self in the globalised context.

References

Benson, Phil, and Terry Lamb. 2020. Autonomy in the age of multilingualism. In *Autonomy in language education: Theory, research and practice*, ed. Manuel Jimenez Raya and Flavia Vieira, 74–88. New York: Routledge. https://doi.org/10.4324/9780429261336-7.

Cavallar, Georg. 2014. Kant and the right of world citizens: An historical interpretation. In *Critique of cosmopolitan reason: Timing and spacing the concept of world citizenship*, ed. Rebecka Lettevall and Kristian Petrov, 141–179. Bern: Peter Lang. https://doi.org/10.3726/978-3-0353-0620-0.

Chayko, Mary. 2021. The practice of identity: Development, expression, performance, form. In *Routledge handbook of digital media and communication*, ed. Leah A. Lievrouw and Brian D. Loader, 115–125. London: Routledge. https://doi.org/10.4324/9781315616551.

Cummins, Jim. 1996. *Negotiating identities: Education for empowerment in a diverse society*. Ontario: California Association for Bilingual Education.

Curry, Oliver Scott, Daniel Austin Mullins, and Harvey Whitehouse. 2019. Is it good to cooperate? Testing the theory of morality-as-cooperation in 60 societies. *Current Anthropology* 60 (1): 47–69. https://doi.org/10.1086/701478.

De Costa, Peter I. 2016a. *The power of identity and ideology in language learning: Designer immigrants learning English in Singapore*. Switzerland: Springer International. https://doi.org/10.1007/978-3-319-30211-9.

De Costa, Peter I. 2016b. Constructing the global citizen an ELF perspective. *Journal of Asian Pacific Communication* 26 (2): 238–259. https://doi.org/10.1075/japc.26.2.04dec.

De Costa, Peter I., and Green-Eneix, Curtis. 2021. Identity in SLA and second language teacher education. In Hassan Mohebbi and Christine Coombe (eds.) *Research questions in language education and applied linguistics: A reference guide*, 537–541. Switzerland AG: Springer. https://doi.org/10.1007/978-3-030-79143-8_94

Elliot, Anthony, and Charles Lamert. 2010. *The new individualism; The emotional costs of globalisation*, 2nd ed. Oxon: Routledge. https://doi.org/10.4324/9780203865705.

Fitriati, Sri Wuli, and Elizabeth Rata. 2021. Language, globalisation, and national identity: A study of English-medium policy and practice in Indonesia. *Journal of Language, Identity and Education* 20 (6): 411–424. https://doi.org/10.1080/15348458.2020.1777865.

Gao, Yihong, Zengyan Jia, and Yan Zhou. 2015. EFL learning and identity development: A longitudinal study in 5 universities in China. *Journal of Language, Identity and Education* 14 (3): 137–158. https://doi.org/10.1080/15348458.2015.1041338.

Gholami, Reza. 2017. The art of self-making: Identity and citizenship education in late-modernity. *British Journal of Sociology of Education* 38 (6): 798–811. https://doi.org/10.1080/01425692.2016.1182006.

Giddens, Anthony. 2006. Modernity and self-identity: Tribulations of the self. In *The discourse reader*, ed. Jaworski Adam and Nikolas Coupland, 415–427. London: Routledge.

Gray, John, and Tom Morton. 2018. *Social interaction and English language teacher identity*. Edinburgh: Edinburgh University Press.

Halliday, Michael A. K. 1994. *An introduction to functional grammar*. London: Edward Arnold.

Harris, Roxy, Constant Leung, and Ben Rampton. 2002. Globalization, diaspora and language education in England. In *Globalization and language teaching*, ed. David Block and Deborah Cameron, 29–46. London: Routledge. https://doi.org/10.4324/9780203193679.

Hegel, Georg Wilhelm Friedrich. 1953. *The philosophy of right*. Translated by Thomas Malcolm Knox. Oxford: Oxford University Press.

Hegel, Georg Wilhelm Friedrich. 1969. *Science of logic*. Translated by Arnold Vincent Miller. London: Allen and Unwin.

Hegel, Georg Wilhelm Friedrich. 1971. *Philosophy of mind: Being part three of the encyclopaedia of philosophical sciences*. Translated by William Wallace. Oxford: Clarendon Press.

Hegel, Georg Wilhelm Friedrich. 1977. *Phenomenology of spirit*. Translated by Arnold Vincent Miller. Oxford: Oxford University Press.

Hegel, Georg Wilhelm Friedrich. 2008. *Outlines of the philosophy of right*. Translated by Stephen Houlgate. Oxford: Oxford University Press.

Ivanič, Roz. 1998. *Writing and identity: The discoursal construction of identity in academic writing*. Amsterdam and Philadelphia: John Benjamins. https://doi.org/10.1075/swll.5

Kanno, Yasuko, and Bonny Norton. 2003. Imagined communities and educational possibilities: Introduction. *Journal of Language, Identity, and Education* 2 (4): 241–249. https://doi.org/10.1207/S15327701JLIE0204_1.

Kant, Immanuel. 1957. *Perpetual peace*. Edited by Lewis White Beck. Englewood Cliffs: Macmillan.

Kant, Immanuel. 1978. *Critique of practical reason*. Translated by Lewis White Beck. Indianapolis: Bobbs-Merrill.

Kant, Immanuel. 2002. *Groundwork of the metaphysics of morals*. Translated by Allen W. Wood. New Haven: Yale University Press.

Liang, Morita. 2015. English, language shift and values shift in Japan and Singapore. *Globalization, Societies and Education* 13 (4): 508–527. https://doi.org/10.1080/14767724.2014.967184.

Liu, Chunge, Mingli Qin, and Ali Ishraq. 2021. The nature of language: On the homogeneity of language and spirit in Hegel's phenomenology of spirit. *Axiomathes* 32 (Suppl 2): 225–240. https://doi.org/10.1007/s10516-021-09595-y.

Lonsonksy, Michael. 2006. *Linguistic turns in modern philosophy*. Cambridge, UK: Cambridge University Press. https://doi.org/10.1017/CBO9780518 1810220.

Lo-Philip, Stephanie Wing Yan and Park, Joseph Sung-Yul. 2015. Imagining self: Diversity of bilingual identity among students of an enrichment. *Journal of Language, Identity and Education* 14 (3): 191–205. https://doi.org/10.1080/15348458.2015.1041344

Lu, Luke. 2020. The (In)significance of race in Singapore's immigration context: Accounts of self-differentiation by academically elite students. *Journal of*

Language, Identity and Education 22 (1): 18–35. https://doi.org/10.1080/15348458.2020.1832494.

Marga, Andrei. 2010. Multilingualism, multiculturalism and autonomy. In Sjur Bergan and Radu Damian (eds.) *Higher education for modern societies—Competences and values*, 49–55. Strasbourg: Council of Europe.

McCarty, Teresa L., Joaquín Noguera, Tiffany S. Lee, and Sheilah E. Nicholas. 2021. 'A viable path for education'—Indigenous-Language immersion and sustainable self-determination. *Journal of Language, Identity and Education* 20 (5): 340–354. https://doi.org/10.1080/15348458.2021.1957681.

Nematzadeh, Azadeh, and Mehry Haddad Narafshan. 2020. Construction and re-construction of identities: A study of learners' personal and L2 identity. *Cogent Psychology* 7 (1): 1823635. https://doi.org/10.1080/23311908.2020.1823635.

Norton, Bonny. 2013. Identity and second language acquisition. In Carol A. Chapelle (ed.) *The encyclopedia of applied linguistic*, 1–8. Malden: Wiley-Blackwell. https://doi.org/10.1002/9781405198431.wbeal0521

Pennycook, Alastair. 2021. *Critical Applied Linguistics: A critical re-introduction*. New York: Routledge.

Phan, Le.-Ha. 2008. *Teaching English as an international language: Identity, resistance and negotiation*. Clevedon: Multilingual Matters.

Poon, Angelia Mui Cheng. 2010. Constructing the cosmopolitan subject: Teaching secondary school literature in Singapore. *Asia Pacific Journal of Education* 30 (1): 31–41. https://doi.org/10.1080/02188790903503577.

Porto, Melina, and Michalinos Zembylas. 2020. Pedagogies of discomfort in foreign language education: Cultivating empathy and solidarity using art and literature. *Language and Intercultural Communication* 20 (4): 356–374. https://doi.org/10.1080/14708477.2020.1740244.

Riley, Philip. 2006. Self-expression and the negotiation of identity in a foreign language. *International Journal of Applied Linguistic* 16 (3): 295–318. https://doi.org/10.1111/j.1473-4192.2006.00120.x.

Rockmore, Tom. 1997. *Cognition: An introduction to Hegel's phenomenology of spirit*. Berkeley: University of California Press.

Rutgers, Dieuwerke, Michael Evans, Linda Fisher, Karen Forbes, Angela Gayton, and Yongcan Liu. 2024. Multilingualism, multilingual identity and academic attainment: Evidence from secondary schools in England. *Journal of Language, Identity and Education*. https://doi.org/10.1080/15348458.2021.1986397.

Ryan, Stephen. 2006. Language learning motivation within the context of globalization: An L2 self within an imagined global community. *Critical Inquiry in Language Studies: An International Journal* 3 (1): 23–45. https://doi.org/10.1207/s15427595cils0301_2.

Saito, Yoshifumi. 2018. Globalization or Anglicization? A dilemma of English language teaching in Japan. In Ryoko Tsuneyoshi (ed.) *Globalization and Japanese exceptionalism in education*, 178–189. Oxon: Routledge. https://doi.org/10.4324/9781315690278

Solomon, Robert C. 1983. *In the spirit of Hegel: A study of G. W. F. Hegel's Phenomenology of Spirit*. New York: Oxford University Press.

Song, Jae Jung. 2013. For whom the bell tolls: Globalization, social class and South Korea's international schools. *Globalization, Societies and Education* 11 (1): 136–159. https://doi.org/10.1080/14767724.2012.750476.

Tarozzi, Massimiliano, and Torrres, Carlos Alberto. 2016. *Global citizenship education and the crises of multiculturalism: Comparative perspectives*. London and New York: Bloomsbury Academic. https://doi.org/10.5040/9781474236003

Torres, Carlos Alberto. 2012. *Education and neoliberal globalization*. New York: Routledge. https://doi.org/10.4324/9780203890738.

Tulgar, Ayşegül Takkaç. 2021. A compromise between global and local: Glocal identity and its effects on pragmatic development. *Journal of Language, Identity and Education* 2021: 1–17. https://doi.org/10.1080/15348458.2021.1956319.

Wu, Manfred Man-fat. 2016. Implications of Hegel's theories of language on second language teaching. *Journal of Curriculum Studies* 48 (3): 346–366. https://doi.org/10.1080/00220272.2016.1151081.

Wu, Manfred Man-fat. 2020. Second language teaching for global citizenship. *Globalisation, Societies and Education* 18 (3): 330–342. https://doi.org/10.1080/14767724.2019.1693349.

Wu, Manfred Man-fat. 2023. *Sublating second language research and practices: Contribution from the Hegelian perspective*. London and New York: Routledge. https://doi.org/10.4324/9781003372240.

Vygotsky, Lev Semenovich. 1986. *Thought and language*. Cambridge: MIT.

Vygotsky, Lev Semenovich. 1987. Thinking and speech. In *The collected works of L.S. Vygotsky: Volume 1, Problems of general psychology*, ed. Robert W. Rieber and Aaron S. Carton, 39–285. New York: Plenum.

CHAPTER 4

Globalisation, L2 Identity, and Morality

Abstract Globalisation exerts profound influences on second language (L2) learning. L2 identity is no exception and deserves special attention, given the role of English as a lingua franca across the world and its key roles in language learning. This chapter continues the discussions of Chapter 3 and examines how globalisation influences the L2 identity of learners from a Hegelian perspective. An evaluation of literature on L2 identity indicates that despite a diversity of theoretical perspectives adopted for research and discussions to date, there has been a lack of attention given to morality, especially the duties to others and their actualisation. From a Hegelian perspective, researching and strengthening L2 identity from the cognitive, social, and instrumental perspectives are inadequate for generating guidance for L2 learners to thrive or at least function properly in the contemporary globalised world. This is because globalisation poses unprecedented challenges to morality, as the mingling of diverse cultures around the globe causes tensions in morality as concluded in Chapters 2 and 3. This paper proposes that morality in Hegelian philosophy be incorporated into research, theoretical development, and implementation of L2 identity. This, from a Hegelian perspective, can facilitate consciousness to declare its conviction, close the gaps and resolve contradictions between moral conscience and the moral reality L2 learners face.

Keywords Globalisation · L2 identity · Hegel · Morality · Social justice

© The Author(s), under exclusive license to Springer Nature   71
Switzerland AG 2024
M. M. Wu, *Globalisation and Second Language Identity*,
https://doi.org/10.1007/978-3-031-68248-3_4

Introduction

Globalisation has been reinforcing the role of English as a lingua franca or as an international language (see Galloway and Rose 2015; O'Regan 2021), and English has been commonly adopted as the language of global culture and international economy. Extensive discussions on cosmopolitanism and global citizenship have been taking place over the past decades (Appiah 2006; Cabrera 2010; Delanty 2019; see also Roldán et al. 2018; Wu et al. in press), and discussions in the L2 field have been focusing on English as an international language and World Englishes, which deal with issues such as the right to the English language, the standard for learner assessments, and the varieties of English around the world. Another major trend in L2 research on globalisation is discussions on global citizenship from an intercultural perspective, with the major tenet that L2 learning is a means for world peace, civil society, and democracy (e.g., Lu and Corbett 2014; Wu 2020).

Language learning shapes and influences learners' identity, and L2 identity has been found to be related to a diverse range of learner variables and learning outcomes (e.g., Neff and Apple 2020). Despite L2 identity being a prominent research topic in the L2 research field, how L2 identity is influenced by globalisation, compared to those focusing on other aspects, has seldom been explored. One often discussed issue in L2 identity and globalisation is the ownership of the English language (Nematzadeh and Narafshan 2020). It is hoped that a more comprehensive theoretical foundation would allow L2 scholars and practitioners to devise more effective curricula and teaching methodology to empower L2 learners for the contemporary globalised world.

After making the recommendations of incorporating human rights in the Kantian sense in Chapter 2 and coupling Kant's human rights with the Hegelian action-oriented fulfilment of duties to others in Chapter 3, this chapter introduces in greater detail how the Hegelian notion of morality can assist learners in overcoming the challenges posed by globalisation. Despite the unpopularity of Hegel among contemporary exponents of globalisation (Browning 2011), Hegel's conceptualisation of morality is highly applicable to research and theoretical development on globalisation. Browning (2011) views that Hegel's (1956) treatment of history as given in his *Philosophy of history* implies that he is a globalist. Hegel (1953) also devotes a section to international law in his *Philosophy of right*. This indicates that like Kant he was aware of the increasing extent of globalisation and the need for the establishment of law for regulating international relations.

From a Hegelian perspective, researching and enhancing L2 identity from the cognitive (e.g., ideal and possible selves), social (such as attitude) and instrumental (such as investment) perspectives are inadequate for generating guidance for L2 learners to thrive or at least function properly in the contemporary globalised world. This is because globalisation places unprecedented challenges on morality, particularly through amplifying social injustice and prejudice (Kamyab and Raby 2023; O'Regan 2021; Pennycook 2021, 2022, 2024). Hegel's notion of morality can effectively fill this gap. Given the influences of globalisation, it is recommended that morality in the Hegelian sense be incorporated into L2 teaching to foster learners' globalised L2 identity. Research, theoretical development, and discussions on L2 identity should also be infused with the Hegelian notion of morality.

The remainder of this chapter consists of four sections. After introducing the key themes which can be drawn from L2 literature on how globalisation influences L2 identity and Hegel's ideas on morality, the inadequacies of the treatments of L2 identity among L2 experts, i.e., neglecting morality, is highlighted. Hegel's notion of morality, which is proposed as a prerequisite for L2 identity to function smoothly in the globalised world in this chapter, is suggested for future theoretical development and research.

Literature on How Globalisation Influences L2 Identity

Before introducing how globalisation exerts demands on contemporary global citizens (Wu 2024), it is necessary to review the literature on globalisation and L2 identity. Details are given below.

Shani (2011) summarises three approaches to the study of globalised identity, namely, the hyperglobalist, the sceptical, and the transformational approaches, which all involve morality. Hyperglobalists view that globalisation has the effect of displacing local identities with a global identity. The displacement means that the moral elements in the local identity will be replaced by foreign one(s). The sceptics, on the other hand, doubt the power of globalisation and view that local identities will remain and will be unaffected by globalisation. The transformationalists, which Shani

(2011) and this chapter endorse, view that both globalisation and localisation are involved in the transformation of identity. Morality, for example, what is regarded as permissible, will be altered with identity transformation. The external social, economic and social forces of globalisation result in the emergence of an imagined external community. Some possible outcomes are adaptation, reconstruction, and strengthening of local identity. Shani (2011) suggests the emergence of new identity elements on top of the traditional ones: "Globalization permits the construction of 'new' syncretic identities which co-exist with 'older' identities based on ethnicity, religion and language with the 'self'" (389). His prediction for future development is that the prevalence of the Internet has made "deterritorialised" diasporic identities possible, but local identities remain to play a major role in social and political life.

Among the empirical research focusing directly on globalisation and L2 identity, Feng and Wang (2020) report the situation of multilingualism and L2 identity among Asian learners. They concluded that the main concern for L2 learners is "maintaining a sense of national identity in the face of globalisation and the increasing use of English as a lingua franca" (161). Wei (2016), on the other hand, investigated the status of globalisation in the L2 identity of local Chinese L2 learners in China. Quantitative data gathered from undergraduates indicate that undergraduates are aware that the English language has the status of a global language, but they lack the awareness of the different varieties of Englishes. English is not a part of their identity, and they regard themselves as learners rather than users of English. This means that globalisation has little influence on the L2 identity of Chinese L2 learners in China as the sceptical approaches (Shani 2011) suggested. A possible Hegelian interpretation of the findings of this study is that little real-life face-to-face encounters with native speakers, which results in a lack of mutual recognition with them and a strong identification with their Chinese culture, are both at work for this group of learners. After becoming "users" instead of "learners" of English, there will be universalisation of the English-speaking cultures and morality on their native Chinese culture. With increasing real-life exchanges (such as during study abroad), learners will feel the tensions (including those on morality) between the English-speaking cultures and their native Chinese cultures as reported by many researchers (e.g., De Costa 2016; Gao et al. 2015; Lo-Philip and Park 2015; Lu 2020; Tulgar 2021) described in Chapter 3.

Both social interactionists and social constructivists emphasise the social influences on L2 identity (Rose and Galloway 2019). Rose and Galloway (2019) as well as Galloway and Rose (2018) contend that despite the difficulties in determining the extent to which language detracts from cultural identity, one thing that can be sure is that language, culture, and identity are inextricably intertwined and mutually affect each other. They (Galloway and Rose 2015) add that some linguistic styles such as American English are commonly regarded as prestigious and therefore the learning of it changes one's identity. Creoles such as those in the Caribbean communities are regarded as a manifestation of national identity and pride. In South Asia, the local variations of English also contribute to the national identity of individuals (for example, Singlish in Singapore).

Kutoba (2018) as well as Kutoba and McKay (2009) adopt a power perspective and view that globalisation has led the West to dominate the rest of the world by means of cultural standardisation and homogenisation. Similarly, Demuth (2018) expresses that globalisation substantially exacerbates the domination of the Western concept of democracy, free market, and consumerism, and resulted in failed states such as Mexico. The incorporation of universal claims (particularly liberal democracy) initiated by the West into the political structure of other parts of the world creates oppression and inequality (see Roldán 2018). Whether to endorse this view requires learners' judgements, thus moral prowess and critical thinking. Despite the ongoing debates on whether the global spread of English is a threat or opportunity (see Wu 2018), the influences of globalisation on L2 identity is a fact that has to be acknowledged. It is not uncommon to see research on how L2 learners struggled for their L2 identity in facing the influence of globalisation (e.g., De Costa 2016). An example is naming, as naming is a political act which involves moral judgements (Ferrini 2020), and naming a learner as bilingual or multilingual has effects on the L2 identity of the learner. The above views reflect that tensions may exist for learners in their L2 identity and moral prowess is needed in maintaining positive attitudes on the varieties of English with the spread of English due to globalisation.

The above summary indicates that as consistently described throughout this book, there has been a lack of attention given to morality, which is proposed to be a key element in L2 identity for learners to overcome the tensions caused by globalisation. The Organization for Economic Cooperation and Development (OECD) (2018) highlights the importance of knowledge, skills, and attitudes for the development of global competence for future generations. Social responsibility extending beyond the local community was stated by elementary school students learning English who participated in research conducted by Davidson and Liu (2020) in Japan. These views show that morality is equally important in addition to knowledge and skills. As language teaching is far from neutral and involves power relations (O'Regan 2021; Phillipson 2013), there is a need for incorporating moral elements in fostering L2 identity of learners. It has been suggested that English language teaching has the duty to perform moral education for sustainability in the context of globalisation (Byram and Wagner 2018; see also Sun and Buripakdi 2021). Hegel's (1953, 1977, 1979, 2008) notion of morality, which is tightly knitted with language, family, community, and politics, is an ideal candidate for harnessing moral elements to enhance theory, research and practice in L2 identity. More importantly, its emphasis on action taking enables morality to be realised in reality.

In the next section, a brief overview of Hegel's socio-anthropological philosophy and his notion of morality will be given. This will be followed by an account of the inadequacies of existing theories on L2 identity in addressing the moral tensions caused by globalisation.

AN OVERVIEW OF HEGEL'S NOTION OF MORALITY

The definition of morality adopted in this book was introduced in Chapter 1. In this fourth chapter of the book, it is worthwhile to revisit the notion of morality from the Hegelian perspective. Hegel (1953) is a strong opponent of the traditional sense of morality (*Moralität*), particularly that of Kant and Fichte, which specifies principles for proper conduct. He criticises *Moralität* as empty in content. Instead, for him, morality refers to ethical life (*Sittlichkeit*), which covers concrete contents. The main themes of ethical life (*Sittlichkeit*) are that the duties to others and actualising these duties by putting them into action are means for closing the gap between the conscience of individuals and reality. This is because taking action objectifies and universalises the subjective will of individuals, enabling the subjective Spirit, the individual mind on a collective scale, to manifest itself in the objective sphere of family, state, and civil society. A concrete example given by Hegel is Antigone (e.g., Gragl 2021), who experienced conflicts between duty to the state and duty to the family. Hegel's conceptualisation of morality, compared to *Moralität*, offers more practical guidelines on how individuals should act. In the remainder of this chapter, how Hegel's morality can harness L2 identity to overcome the challenges brought by globalisation will be introduced.

The actualisation of the duties to others influences the identity construction of individuals, as it provides real-life content for individuals to construct and reconstruct their self-identity. This process of morality involves interactions with others and the inevitable use of language. In fact, it is commonly regarded that language is the existence of Spirit at large, ethical spirit, cultural world, moral consciousness, and conscience (Liu et al. 2021). Facing the trend of globalisation, contemporary L2 learners no longer interact with other individuals in their local community only. It is common for individuals to have opportunities to take actions to carry out their duties to others for members of the global community with the aid of the L2 (e.g., in the recent movements of "#MeToo" and "#BlackLivesMatter"). These interactions will inevitably influence how individuals view themselves as L2 learners. In short, morality (*Sittlichkeit*, or ethical life), L2 learning, L2 identity, and globalisation are intimately related to each other. Through taking actions to actualise one's duties to others, both the individual and collective self-consciousness can transform itself from the state of "*being-in-itself*" to "*being-for-itself*" (Hegel 1977).

L2 identity research and discussions are more anthropological in nature. Therefore, in this section, references will be made to Hegel's main ideas in his major published work, the *Phenomenology of Spirit* (*PhS*) (Hegel 1977), which covers more on both anthropology and morality.

Hegel's socio-anthropological philosophy as described in his *PhS* begins with individual consciousness, which is part of the collective human consciousness. The primitive mode of collective consciousness is sense perception, in which an individual has little knowledge of the surroundings and awareness of himself other than those obtained from the senses. Through repeated encounters with other individuals (or "consciousnesses"), an individual begins to differentiate himself from others, gains awareness of himself, and becomes self-conscious through mutual recognition. The most renowned stage (or "moment" in Hegel's terminology) is the master and slave relationship, in which a subject who gives up his freedom for his life in a life-and-death struggle between him and another consciousness becomes the slave, while the winner of the struggle becomes the master. However, through fear, anxiety, labour, and alienation in this unequal power relationship, the slave finally gains self-consciousness or wisdom. The above account aligns well with the post-structural view, that the development and implementation of L2 identity involve struggles and negotiation of meanings on the part of learners (Wu 2023).

Self-consciousness then progresses to higher and more advanced moments of development through the dialectical mechanisms of posit-edness, negation, synthesis and sublation, in which elements of more basic levels are preserved in the next higher levels (e.g., Hegel 1969). Consciousness progresses from the intrapersonal level to become self-consciousness at the interpersonal level and progresses dialectically to the collective level with increasing self-knowledge, or in Hegel's terminology, from the "*individual-in-himself*" to the "*individual-for-himself*". On the collective level, one moment related to morality is the stage in which self-consciousness faces struggles between the law of the heart and reality. Upon resolving the gaps between their conscience and the reality, a shared subjectivity, including morality, is achieved.

The resolution of the contradictions in this stage paves the way for the ethical life (*Sittlichkeit*) which is characterised by individual members being fully recognised and being well aware of their rights and duties in civil society, with morality endowed with concrete content. In the ulti-mate stage of Absolute Freedom, consciousness has transformed from the inchoate stage of "*being-in-itself*" to "*being-for-itself*", and it possesses Absolute Knowledge, or knowledge that is all-encompassing and free of contradictions (Solomon 1983). In all these moments, Hegel makes frequent references to language, emphasising its role in externalising inner subjectivities of consciousness, enabling dialectic to operate, achieving universality, and enabling the Spirit to unfold itself to the objective collective human entity.

HEGEL ON LANGUAGE AND MORALITY

Hegel did not discuss how L2 learning contributes to morality. However, he (Hegel 1977) points out an important function of language, that it distances the individual from himself and externalises his meanings to achieve universality and to enable the development of self. According to him (Hegel 1977), language is self-consciousness existing for others, is the self that separates itself from itself. It perceives itself just as it is perceived by others.

In his discussions on morality, Hegel (1977) focuses on the discrepancies and contradictions between morality and reality or duty and actuality, which cause struggles for self-consciousness on its progression to Absolute Knowing (for example, in the section "C. Spirit That is Certain of Itself. Morality" of *PhS*). There are discrepancies and contradictions between the moral view of the world, which exist in the relation between the absoluteness of morality and the absoluteness of Nature (Hegel 1977, §600: 365). There is a contradiction between morality and Nature, and it is "contradiction of a task which is to remain a task and yet ought to be fulfilled" (§603: 369).

Hegel (1977) treats pure duty as the core characteristic of morality, and points out the importance of combining it with actuality, i.e. acting out and fulfilling pure duty through influencing the actual world:

> ... in the Notion of the moral self-consciousness the two aspects, pure duty and actuality, are explicitly joined in a single unity, and consequently the one, like the other, is expressly without a being of its own, but is only a moment, or is superseded ... [consciousness] places pure duty in a being other than itself, i.e. it posits pure duty in a being other than itself, i.e. it posits pure duty partly as something existing only in thought, partly as something that is not valid in and for itself; rather it is the non-moral [consciousness] that is held to be perfect. Equally, it gives itself the character of a consciousness whose actuality, not being in conformity with duty, is superseded and qua superseded, or in the idea of absolute Being, no longer contradicts morality (Hegel 1977, §610: 371).

In fact, pure duty is the self of consciousness, which is being and actuality, viz pure knowing (Hegel 1977, §632: 384), and is the simple selfhood and self-identity (Hegel 1977, §646: 393). It is one of the overarching themes of this book.

Hegel (1977) adds that morality in and for itself is in another being, and pure duty has validity only with the existence of another being:

> Pure duty has also in point of fact validity only in another being, not in the morality consciousness. Although to the latter it seems that pure morality alone has validity, the position must be put in another way, for it is at the same time a natural consciousness (§627: 380).

Globalisation involves interactions among individuals, is part of nature in the development of the collective human entity, and therefore involves morality: "[T]here are certainly ought to be action, absolute duty ought to be expressed in the whole of Nature, and the moral law to become natural law" (Hegel 1977, §619: 375). This implies that pure duty, the key element of morality, is a prerequisite for successful globalisation. In order to function effectively in the globalised community, an individual needs to be equipped with pure duty on globalisation.

The feature of morality being internal in nature also renders it highly suitable for being cultivated by L2 learning:

> Morality is the 'in-itself', the purely implicit element; if it is to be actual, the final purpose of the world cannot be fulfilled; rather the moral conscious-ness must exist on its own account and find itself confronted by a nature opposed to it … Moral self-consciousness asserts that its purpose is pure, is independent of inclinations and impulses, which implies that it has eliminated within itself sensuous purposes (Hegel 1977, §622: 377).

In summary, from the Hegelian perspective, language is a key element of L2 identity, and language constitutes morality. Morality, particularly pure duty and its actualisation, are parts of global L2 identity. The inad-equacies of existing literature on L2 identity in addressing globalisation are introduced in the next section. How Hegelian philosophy can over-come these inadequacies of past discussions on L2 identity in the context of globalisation will also be suggested.

Lack of Recommendations for Globalised L2 Identity and Hegel's Morality as a Solution

A major theme of this chapter and this book at large is that globalisa-tion places unprecedented demands on morality such as social injustice (in terms of traditional inequality of gender, ethnicity, economics, and politics) (Kamyab and Raby 2023; Pennycook 2021; O'Regan 2021) and prejudice (such as cultural relativism, nationalism, and ethnic stereo-types) (Caluori et al. 2021) due to tensions in morality resulting from the mingling of diverse cultures in the world and increasing interactions among individuals from different parts of the world. The social injus-tice caused by internationalisation of higher education has well been documented, and counter policy in countries such as Canada has been implemented (see Kamyab and Raby 2023). These moral issues are seldom addressed in existing literature on L2 identity, and the Hegelian perspective offers ideal solutions to fill this theoretical lacuna.

Roldán (2018) remarks that globalisation is a concept that is empty in content. According to him (Roldán 2018), one salient missing component which has been neglected in the discussions on globalisation is ethics, and the parallel lack of attention given to ethics is found in discussions on L2 identity. Therefore, this book proposes that morality be taken into consideration in research and discussions on L2 identity. In the same vein, Méndez (2018) highlights that values and principles form moral identity, and moral identity determines societal consensus on justice. In this section, how Hegelian morality can harness learners in terms of their L2 identity in facing the tensions generated by globalisation as a continuation of the discussions undertaken in Chapters 2 and 3 are introduced.

Hegelian Morality for Overcoming Inequality

Globalisation has brought three phenomena that give rise to tensions on morality (Méndez 2018). The first is hypersocialisation and hypertextuality. Hypersocialisation refers to the possibility of action that detaches from space and time, while hypertextuality refers to the use of the appearance of audio, video, and text all at the same time. The second phenomenon is interdependence, meaning that decisions made in a state can have influence on other parts of the world. The ubiquity and high speed of exchanges across time and culture inevitably bring tensions for values and morality, as individuals in the globalised world are constantly flooded with conflicting views and values. The third phenomenon that may be caused by differences in cultural perceptions is the exercise of power and reproduction of inequalities facilitated by interconnection and interdependence. All these phenomena indicate that as has been mentioned throughout this book, individuals need to be equipped with a set of globalised morality as part of their identity in order to function effectively as global citizens.

The possible inequalities amplified by globalisation caused by cultural differences on equality, morality and value require individuals and government the moral prowess and critical thinking to overcome the challenges and improve world order. The effects of globalisation in amplifying inequality have been revealed from different angles (Chayko 2021; Heid and Larch 2016; Hung 2021; Mikander 2016; Van Rensburg et al. 2020). Two effects of globalisation in terms of income reported by Hung (2021) are the expansion of internal inequality in poor and rich countries and the stagnation of income of the working class. However, evidence has supported that globalisation has narrowed the income gap between countries, despite the fact that there has been an export of inequalities in different forms from the rich to poor countries, for example, in terms of work arrangements and salary (see Hung 2021). Globalisation influences national policies, which in turn affects economic inequality (Mikander 2016). Evidence on globalisation causing unemployment (Heid and Larch 2016) and strengthening of the bond between power and economic status (with the rich becoming richer and politically more powerful) (Hurst et al. 2017) has been revealed. Van Rensburg et al. (2020) identified augmentation of income gaps between male and female workers engaged in international trade caused by globalisation, and for Tarozzi and Torres (2016) a by-product of globalisation is that it offers unlimited opportunities to an extremely small number of people, which exacerbates inequalities.

Globalisation intensifies differentiation in terms of ethnic identity, class, and gender, and at the same time gives rise to new inequalities because of the new world order such as the North–South divide of nation states, hence fostering global injustice (Di Castro 2018). It has been suggested that the global use of digital technology amplifies inequality and makes inequality visible on a global scale (Chayko 2021). With increasing awareness of global inequality in different aspects, individuals experience the gaps between their conscience and the moral reality described by Hegel (1977) introduced in the last section. Facing amplifying inequalities, the moral prowess harnessed by cultivation of L2 identity enables individuals to take action to resolve the tensions.

Hegelian Morality for Overcoming Prejudice

Caluori et al. (2021) identified the relationships between globalisation and prejudice, which are proposed in this book as related to a lack of awareness of duties to others. Globalisation has caused an increase in prejudice in countries with high economic inequality and a decrease in prejudice in countries with low economic inequality. Caluori et al.'s (2021) findings bridge the research gap of the lack of empirical evidence for the need for morality, especially pure duty and its actualisation from a Hegelian (1977, 2008) perspective. Globalisation heightens the level of prejudice against others of other races, religions, and languages in countries with high economic inequality, and this is detrimental to human morality. As morality is part of L2 identity, this means that L2 identity will be adversely affected and need to be transformed (Shani 2011). Negative experiences such as discrimination and fear of violence which are emotional in nature may become parts of the identity of individuals. Measures need to be taken to inculcate a positive morality in L2 learners, especially by inculcating a sense of duty to other members of the global community and its actualisation, as described by Hegel (1977, 2008).

Critical Applied Linguistics for Social Justice

The Critical Applied Linguistics perspective (Pennycook 2001, 2021, 2022, 2024), which shares many commonalities with the Kantian and Hegelian perspectives, describes how the global spread of English exacerbates social injustice in different parts of the world regardless of gender, social class, and ethnicity. Inequalities are caused by domination, disparity, discrimination, difference, and desire. The dominance of a normative language standard of English results in Eurocentric and myopic view (Guilherme 2018), and L2 learners need to be empowered in terms of morality to rectify the inequalities caused by globalisation.

Concurring with Hegel (1977), Pennycook (2001, 2021, 2022, 2024) advocates for taking actions to implement the moral commitment of L2 teaching for correcting injustice, and concludes that instead of being static and features possessed by individual, identity is something which we perform. The performative nature of identity emphasised by Pennycook (2001, 2021, 2022, 2024) is an important reminder for L2 researchers on the dynamic and fluid nature of L2 identity described by the post-structuralist approaches and this book. An action-oriented perspective to L2 identity is particularly relevant for globalisation because globalisation's transnational social movements give rise to new forms of social and political participation for individuals (Gaventa and Tandon 2010), for example, the "#MeToo" movement which has generated resonances across the globe since 2017 and the "#BlackLivesMatter" since 2013. Taking action has also been promoted in many contexts, for example, English learning classrooms in China (Sun 2023).

Equally critical but from a macro perspective, O'Regan (2021) analysed how the historical global spread of the English language contributes to the never-ending accumulation of capital and reproduces inequalities on a global scale. Through increasing commercialisation and world trade, English has been able to enjoy the status of a free-rider of international economic activities and dominates. The free-ride privilege of Anglophone world is still acute today, and it has accelerated economic inequality (Finkbeiner and White 2017).

Diversity of Identities and Critical Literacy

Globalisation is dominating in nature, and is a "negative inheritance" of the Enlightenment (which ironically was the birthplace of Hegel's philosophy) which focused on rationality, teleology, continuity, and perfection (Roldán 2018). These forces inevitably influence the development of L2 identity. Roldán (2018) contends that "it is an urgent task to rehabilitate politics and produce new collective actors, in accordance with concept such as isogoria and isonomy, including the necessary gender perspective" (115).[1] Resonating Roldán (2018) and Shani (2011), Méndez (2018) argues for the idea of the "diversity of identities" because, in the contemporary globalisation context, conventional national citizenship is unable to account for globalised politics. According to him, "diversity of identities" is more suitable for discussions on who is the subject of justice, as this idea takes into consideration cultural diversity. Despite the potential heuristic value of the idea of "diversity of identities", no concrete details are given by Méndez (2018). More efforts are required for this idea to take off in the academic and political arenas. What is relevant to the focus of this chapter is that the diversity of identities needs a common moral foundation, and Hegel's (1977) pure duty and its actualisation are highly pertinent.

Increasing globalisation has highlighted the importance of critical literacy on the seemingly democratic global value which exists on the surface (Finkbeiner and White 2017). Loader (2021) even argues that digital media is detrimental to democracy because it is very often being manipulated. According to Finkbeiner and White (2017), there is a need for awareness that digital social networks are owned by a few, and

students need to learn about the pluses and minuses of social networks. They should also become aware of language change in and through the

---

[1] Isogoria refers to equal right of public speech, and isonomy equal right before the law.

media with respect to the oral and written mode as well as emoticons and discourse style. They need to re-learn the distinction between public vs. private, official vs. non-official discourse, learn to deal with cyberbullying and apply proper netiquette. Furthermore, gender issues play a role in online communication (9).

From a Hegelian perspective, the above recommendations of the diversity of identities and critical literacy should be based on a sense of duty to others and its actualisation.

In order for nation states to maintain their economic competitiveness in the face of information flows and knowledge networks that surpass the territorial controls of the state, they have had to opt for the formation of regional blocs (Di Castro 2018). Garcia (2021) is of the view that in the current globalised world, digital literacy is intimately related to the issues of equity, pedagogy, and power. In line with the focus of this chapter, he (Garcia 2021) views that literacy is embodied, social and interpersonally connected, and is therefore intimately related to L2 identity. Globalisation "is a concept with deep roots in communication and media scholarship" (Flew 2021: 350). In today's participatory culture and with the penetration of communication technology, individuals need to redefine the new conglomeration of audience, which is entirely different from the traditional audience (Chayko 2021; Garcia 2021). A new basis of morality is essential, and the Hegelian notion of morality is an ideal choice to fill this gap, given its foundation of mutual recognition and its emphasis on action taking. In the third and fourth sections of this chapter, it was mentioned that mutual recognition as represented by the master and slave dialectic forms the basis of morality in Hegel's philosophy, and morality is also only valid with the existence of others. As L2 identity is defined and influenced by reciprocal interpersonal relations with others, we can expect L2 identity in the contemporary world to have a unique make-up. Digital literacy begins within the bodies of individuals and is connected to inequality (Garcia 2021), and the element of embodiment in digital literacy resonates with Hegel's action-oriented morality.

National Borders for Cultural Identity Preservation

Hegel's philosophy contributes to a new understanding of personal identity in terms of national borders. The study of borders has been neglected in political theory. Libertarians, such as Steiner (1994), treat national borders as free from morality and as merely physical boundaries between lands of different nations (Brown 2011). Despite being arbitrarily determined, geographical national borders have value in preserving cultural identities. Identity is about difference, and it distinguishes one state from another and performs the function of maintaining these differences. Given this premise, a borderless world would pose problems for identity. Paraphrasing Hegel (2008), Brown (2011) expresses that individuals need a competitive, public environment outside the protective family environment to develop themselves. The state provides such an environment, in which "the inequalities of civil society are countered by the notion of equal citizenship and (perhaps) an equal contribution to the general arrangements of a society" (Brown 2011: 130).

Given the above view, the Hegelian perspective would argue for the maintenance of physical national borders. Borders in the cyberworld cannot establish and maintain identities as effectively as the physical community can (Brown 2011). However, globalisation is replacing the diverse identities of the older generation with those of the new, universal and homogenised identities for the next generation, a tenet shared by the transformationalists (Shani 2011) and this book. The emphases on physical national borders and the protection of cultural heritage (including morality) are beneficial for the development and maintenance of L2 identity for globalisation.

The effects of globalisation are also manifested in the emergence of non-state bodies represented by the United Nations. These bodies function as sources for identity (including that of the L2) formation on a global scale, particularly through its UNESCO for cultural preservation (UNESCO 2023). The lack of consideration given to morality in the discussions of borders in political theory has caused embarrassment in the field, and Brown (2011) calls for the development of new perspectives, as normative theories developed in the past are no longer applicable to today's globalised world. In a study conducted in Thailand, it was found that local value systems are maintained, reasserted, and reshaped dynamically by the force of globalisation (McKenzie and Jensen 2024). Proposals such as the promotion of morality from the Hegelian perspective—a sense of duty to others and its actualisation—offered in this book are potentially valuable in overcoming the embarrassment.

Global Mutual Recognition

In addition to advocating for morality, Browning (2011) also calls for attention to the significance of global mutual recognition in the globalised world, which is integral to L2 identity. According to him,

> Hegel takes individual states to interact with one another, registering their identities via this mutual recognition, and in doing so, he identifies how a sense of the world in the historical process develops. Hegel's notion of this sense of the world renders it dependent upon its historical and recognitive conceptualisation. It seems on the surface of it counter-intuitive to attribute a concept of globalisation to theorists who, like Hegel, do not formulate an express theory of globalisation (49–50).

Hegel (1953), in his discussions on international law, echoes Kant's idea of perpetual peace, and regards a state as an autonomous individual in civil society. He contends mutual recognition among states is significant for maintaining healthy international relations. This type of mutual recognition homogenises moralities of nations, simultaneously highlighting the differences among them in terms of morality. This topic deserves discussion in a separate book for discussions, and is a fruitful area for future development in global theories.

On the interpersonal level, the L2 enables an individual to communicate with people of other linguistic communities, not necessarily English-speaking communities. This allows mutual recognition across the globe to take place. This is especially true with the technological advancement in electronic communications, which allows mutual recognition to take place across space and time at high speed through enhanced social presence (Chayko 2021). Technology provides countless (albeit standardised) ways for expressing identity, and the outcome is a heightened level of self-consciousness for learners.

Despite playing a less significant role in social solidarity and morality compared to the L1, the L2 plays a significant role in the universalisation and objectification of meanings, culture, and morality between the local community of learners, the target communities (i.e., the English-speaking countries), and other linguistic communities. L2 identity has been found to be attached to cultural context (Han 2021; Nematzadeh and Narafshan 2020). As culture and morality can hardly be separated, L2 identity is inevitably related to morality. Neoliberalism, which has been exported by the West in the process of globalisation, is based on rationality (Demuth 2018). This means that many cultural and moral elements in non-Western cultures which are regarded as irrational in Western cultures will be attacked or discarded with the increasing extent of globalisation. The tensions created by globalisation on this aspect gave rise to an emerging trend related to morality such as heritage preservation (e.g., Al-Hammadi and Alkaabi 2021). This means that despite the importance of mutual recognition achieved by the L2, there is a limit for mutual identification among states and the difference between states should be respected.

Conclusion

This chapter has highlighted a major theme of this book of the lack of attention given to morality in globalisation for L2 identity. A brief sketch of Hegel's philosophy and morality has been introduced, and the relevance of Hegel's notion of morality for infusing L2 identity with the moral prowess to overcome the challenges posed by globalisation has been proposed. Morality characterised by a sense of duty to others, taking actions to actualise duties, and mutual recognition on both the state and individual levels is called for. This book proposes that morality in Hegelian philosophy be incorporated into research, theoretical development and implementation of L2 identity. This, from a Hegelian perspective, can facilitate consciousness to declare its conviction, close the gaps and resolve contradictions between moral conscience and the moral reality L2 learners face.

The review of literature on L2 identity in this chapter indicates that despite the diversity of theoretical perspectives adopted for research and discussions to date, there has been a lack of attention given to morality, especially the duties to others and its actualisation proposed by Hegel. The discussions on the amplification of inequalities, augmentation of interdependence and prejudice, and the need for mutual recognition among nations, which are some of the outcomes of globalisation, need morality as their foundation in order for L2 identity to flourish.

References

Al-Hammadi, Mariam I., and Ibrahim M. Alkaabi. 2021. Socio-economic development, globalization and the need for heritage policy in Qatar: Case study. *Open Journal of Social Sciences* 9 (3): 435–456. https://doi.org/10.4236/jss.2021.93028.

Appiah, Kwame Anthony. 2006. *Cosmopolitanism. Ethics in a world of strangers.* London: Penguin Books.

Brown, Chris. 2011. Borders and identity in international political theory. In Mathias Albert, David Jacobson, and Yosef Lapid (eds.) *Identities, borders, orders—Rethinking international relations theory,* 117–136. Minnesota: University of Minnesota Press. https://doi.org/10.1017/S0003055402900365

Browning, Gary. 2011. *Global theory from Kant to Hardt and Negri. International political theory series.* London: Palgrave Macmillan. https://doi.org/10.1057/9780230308541_3

Byram, Michael, and Manuela Wagner. 2018. Making a difference: Language teaching for intercultural and international dialogue. *Foreign Language Annals* 51 (1): 140–151. https://doi.org/10.1111/flan.12319.

Cabrera, Luis. 2010. *The practice of global citizenship.* Cambridge: Cambridge University Press. https://doi.org/10.1017/CBO9780511762833.

Caluori, Nava, Brown-Iannuzzi, Jazmin L., and Cipolli III, William. 2021. Economic inequality shapes the relationship between globalization and prejudice. *Social Psychological and Personality Science* 12 (6): 1082–1091. https://doi.org/10.1177/1948550620960929

Chayko, Mary. 2021. The practice of identity: Development, expression, performance, form. In Leah A. Lievrouw and Brian D. Loader (eds.) *Routledge handbook of digital media and communication,* 115–125. London and New York: Routledge. https://doi.org/10.4324/9781315616551

Davidson, Rachel, and Yongcan Liu. 2020. Reaching the world outside: Cultural representation and perceptions of global citizenship in Japanese elementary school English textbooks. *Language, Culture and Curriculum* 33 (1): 32–49. https://doi.org/10.1080/07908318.2018.1560460.

De Costa, Peter I. 2016. *The power of identity and ideology in language learning: designer immigrants learning English in Singapore.* Switzerland: Springer International. https://doi.org/10.1007/978-3-319-30211-9

Delanty, Gerard, ed. 2019. *Routledge international handbook of cosmopolitanism studies.* New York: Routledge. https://doi.org/10.4324/9781351028905.

Demuth, Constanze. 2018. Liberalism's all-inclusive promise of freedom and its illiberal effects: A critique of the concept of globalization. In Concha Roldán, Daniel Brauer, and Johannes Rohbeck (eds.) *Philosophy of globalization*, 63–77. Berlin and Boston: Walter de Gruyter. https://doi.org/10.1515/978311 0492415-006

Di Castro, Elisabetta. 2018. Globalization, inequalities and justice. In Concha Roldán, Daniel Brauer, and Johannes Rohbeck (eds.) *Philosophy of globalization*, 123–136. Berlin and Boston: Walter de Gruyter. https://doi.org/10. 1515/9783110492415-010

Feng, Teng Mark, and Lixun Wang. 2020. *Identity, motivation, and multilingual education in Asian contexts*. London: Bloomsbury Academic. https:// doi.org/10.1080/02607476.2021.1958656.

Ferrini, Cinzia. 2020. Freedom through otherness: Hegel's lesson on human subjectivity and intersubjectivity. In *Human diversity in context*, ed. Cinzia Ferrini, 169–207. Trieste: University of Trieste.

Finkbeiner, Claudia H. and White, Joanna. 2017. Language awareness and multilingualism: A historical overview. In Jasone Cenoz, Durk Gorter, and Stephen May (eds.) *Language awareness and multilingualism*, 1–13. Cham: Springer. https://doi.org/10.1007/978-3-319-02325-0_1-2

Flew, Terry. 2021. Globalization and post-globalization. In Leah A. Lievrouw and Brian D. Loader (eds.) *Routledge handbook of digital media and communication*, 350–362. London and New York: Routledge. https://doi.org/10. 4324/9781315616551

Galloway, Nicola, and Heath Rose. 2015. *Introducing Global Englishes*. London and New York: Routledge. https://doi.org/10.4324/9781315734347.

Galloway, Nicola, and Heath Rose. 2018. Incorporating Global Englishes into the ELT classroom. *ELT Journal* 72 (1): 3–14. https://doi.org/10.1093/ elt/ccx010.

Gao, Yihong, Zengyan Jia, and Yan Zhou. 2015. EFL learning and identity development: A longitudinal study in 5 universities in China. *Journal of Language, Identity & Education* 14 (3): 137–158. https://doi.org/10. 1080/15348458.2015.1041338.

Garcia, Antero. 2021. Digital literacies in a wireless world. In Leah A. Lievrouw and Brian D. Loader (eds.) *Routledge handbook of digital media and communication*, 143–153. London and New York: Routledge. https://doi.org/10. 4324/9781315616551

Gaventa, John, and Rrajesh Tandon. 2010. *Globalizing citizens: New dynamics of inclusion and exclusion*. London and New York: Zed Books Ltd.

Gragl, Paul. 2021. Hegel's Antigone: The birth of the constitution from the spirit of tragedy. *ICL Journal* 15 (4): 413–434. https://doi.org/10.1515/ icl-2021-0020.

Guilherme, Manuela. 2018. 'Glocal languages': The 'glocalness' and the 'localness' of world languages. In Simon Coffey and Ursula Wingate (eds.) *New directions for research in foreign language education*, 79–96. New York: Routledge. https://doi.org/10.4324/9781315561561

Han, Yiting. 2021. Exploring language learners' identity development in intercultural contexts: Current landscape and ways forward. *Journal of Second Language Acquisition and Teaching* 27: 4–14.

Hegel, Georg Wilhelm Friedrich. 1953. *The philosophy of right*. Translated by Thomas Malcolm Knox. Oxford: Oxford University Press.

Hegel, Georg Wilhelm Friedrich. 1956. *The philosophy of history*. New York: Dover.

Hegel. Georg Wilhelm Friedrich. 1969. *Science of logic*. Translated by Arnold Vincent Miller. London: Allen and Unwin.

Hegel, Georg Wilhelm Friedrich. 1977. *Phenomenology of spirit*. Translated by Arnold Vincent Miller. Oxford: Oxford University Press.

Hegel, Georg Wilhelm Friedrich. 1979. *System of ethical life and first philosophy of spirit*. Translated by Thomas Malcolm Knox. Albany: State University of New York Press.

Hegel, Georg Wilhelm Friedrich. 2008. *Outlines of the philosophy of right*. Translated by Thomas Malcolm Knox. Oxford: Oxford University Press.

Heid, Benedikt, and Mario Larch. 2016. Gravity with unemployment. *Journal of International Economics* 101 (1): 70–85. https://doi.org/10.1016/j.jinteco.2016.03.008.

Hung, Ho-Fung. 2021. Recent trends in global economic inequality. *Annual Review of Sociology* 47: 349–368. https://doi.org/10.1146/annurev-soc-090320-105810.

Hurst, Charles E., Heather Fitz Gibbon, and Anne M. Nurse. 2017. *Social inequality: Forms, causes, and consequences*. New York and Oxon: Routledge. https://doi.org/10.4324/9781003184966.

Kamyab, Shahrzad, and Rosalind Latiner Raby, eds. 2023. *Unintended consequences of internationalization in higher education: Comparative international perspectives on the impacts of policy and practice*. New York: Routledge. https://doi.org/10.4324/9781003189916.

Kubota, Ryuko. 2018. Unpacking research and practice in world Englishes and second language acquisition. *World Englishes* 37: 93–105. https://doi.org/10.1111/weng.12305.

Kubota, Ryuko, and Sandra McKay. 2009. Globalization and language learning in rural Japan: The role of English in the local linguistic ecology. *TESOL Quarterly* 43 (4): 593–619. https://doi.org/10.1002/j.1545-7249.2009.tb00188.x.

Lo-Philip, Stephanie Wing Yan and Park, Joseph Sung-Yul. 2015. Imagining self: Diversity of bilingual identity among students of an enrichment. *Journal of Language, Identity & Education* 14 (3): 191–205. https://doi.org/10.1080/15348458.2015.1041344

Loader, Brian D. 2021. What remains of digital democracy? Contemporary political cleavages and democratic practices. In Leah A. Lievrouw and Brian D. Loader (eds.) *Routledge handbook of digital media and communication*, 177–190. London and New York: Routledge. https://doi.org/10.4324/9781315616551

Liu, Chunge, Mingli Qin, and Ali Ishraq. 2021. The nature of language: On the homogeneity of language and spirit in Hegel's phenomenology of spirit. *Axiomathes* 32 (Suppl 2): 225–240. https://doi.org/10.1007/s10516-021-09595-y.

Lu, Luke. 2020. The (In)significance of race in Singapore's immigration context: Accounts of self-differentiation by academically elite students. *Journal of Language, Identity & Education* 22 (1): 18–35. https://doi.org/10.1080/15348458.2020.1832494.

Lu, Peih-ying and Corbett, John. 2014. An intercultural approach to second language education and citizenship. In Jane Jackson (ed.) *Routledge handbook of language and intercultural communication*. South Carolina: Routledge. https://doi.org/10.4324/9780203805640

McKenzie, Jessica, and Lene Arnett Jensen. 2024. The globalization and localization of moral values: A cultural-developmental study of adolescents and their parents. *International Journal of Behavioral Development*. https://doi.org/10.1177/01650254231222418.

Méndez, Alberto Ruiz. 2018. Who are the subjects of justice in a globalized world? From the 'unidimensional identity' to the 'diversity of identities'. In Concha Roldán, Daniel Brauer, and Johannes Rohbeck (eds.) *Philosophy of globalization*, 153–166. Berlin and Boston: Walter de Gruyter. https://doi.org/10.1515/9783110492415-012

Mikander, Pia. 2016. Globalization as continuing colonialism: Critical global citizenship education in an unequal world. *Journal of Social Science Education* 15 (2): 70–79. https://doi.org/10.4119/UNIBI/jsse-v15-i2-1475.

Neff, Peter, and Matthew Apple. 2020. Short-term and long-term study abroad: The impact on language learners' intercultural communication, L2 confidence, and sense of L2 self. *Journal of Multilingual and Multicultural Development* 44 (7): 572–588. https://doi.org/10.1080/01434632.2020.1847125.

Nematzadeh, Azadeh, and Mehry Haddad Narafshan. 2020. Construction and re-construction of identities: A study of learners' personal and L2 identity. *Cogent Psychology* 7 (1): 1823635. https://doi.org/10.1080/23311908.2020.1823635.

O'Regan, John. 2021. *Global English and political economy*. Oxon: Routledge. https://doi.org/10.4324/9781315749334.

Pennycook, Alastair. 2001. *Critical Applied Linguistics: A critical introduction.* Mahwah: Lawrence Erlbaum. https://doi.org/10.4324/9781410600790.

Pennycook, Alastair. 2021. *Critical Applied Linguistics: A critical re-introduction.* New York: Routledge. https://doi.org/10.4324/9781003090571.

Pennycook, Alastair. 2022. Critical applied linguistics in the 2020s. *Critical Inquiry in Language Studies* 19 (1): 1–21. https://doi.org/10.1080/154 27587.2022.2030232.

Pennycook, Alastair. 2024. Critical applied linguistics. *Oxford research encyclopedias, Linguistics.* Retrieved 5 April 2024, from https://doi.org/10.1093/acr efore/9780199384655.001.0001/acrefore-9780199384655-e-1022

Phillipson, Robert. 2013. Linguistic imperialism. In Carol A. Chapelle (ed.) *The encyclopedia of Applied Linguistics*, 3470–3476. London: Blackwell. https://doi.org/10.1002/9781405198431.wbeal0718

Roldán, Concha. 2018. The thinning and deformation of ethical and political concepts in the era of globalization. In Concha Roldán, Daniel Brauer, and Johannes Rohbeck (eds.), *Philosophy of globalization*, 109–122. Berlin and Boston: Walter de Gruyter. https://doi.org/10.1515/9783110492415-009

Roldán, Concha, Daniel Brauer, and Johannes Rohbeck, eds. 2018. *Philosophy of globalization.* Berlin and Boston: Walter de Gruyter. https://doi.org/10.1515/9783110492415.

Rose, Heath, and Nicola Galloway. 2019. *Global Englishes for language teaching.* Cambridge: Cambridge University Press. https://doi.org/10.1017/978131 6678343.

Shani, Giorgio. 2011. Identity-politics in the global age. In Anthony Elliot (ed.) *Routledge handbook of identity studies*, 380–396. London and New York: Routledge. https://doi.org/10.4324/9781315626024

Solomon, Robert C. 1983. *In the spirit of Hegel: A study of G. W. F. Hegel's Phenomenology of spirit.* New York: Oxford University Press. https://doi.org/10.2307/2185140

Steiner, Hillel. 1994. *An essay on rights.* Oxford: Blackwell. https://doi.org/10.2307/2956454.

Sun, Lina. 2023. Cultivating critical global citizens through secondary EFL education: A case study of mainland China. *Literacy* 57 (3): 249–261. https://doi.org/10.1111/lit.12314.

Sun, Tingting and Buripakdi, Adcharawan. 2021. Scrutiny of global citizenship in Chinese elementary school English textbooks and teachers' practices during COVID-19 pandemic. *Asia Pacific Journal of Educators and Education* 36 (2): 257–280. https://doi.org/10.21315/apjee2021.36.2.13

Tarozzi, Massimiliano, and Torrres, Carlos Alber. 2016. *Global citizenship education and the crises of multiculturalism: Comparative perspectives.* London and New York: Bloomsbury Academic. https://doi.org/10.5040/978147 4236003

The Organization for Economic Cooperation and Development. 2018. *Preparing our youth for an inclusive and sustainable world: The OECD PISA global competence framework*. Paris: OECD.

Tulgar, Ayşegül Takkaç. 2021. A compromise between global and local: Glocal identity and its effects on pragmatic development. *Journal of Language, Identity & Education* 2021: 1–17. https://doi.org/10.1080/15348458.2021.1956319.

Van Rensburg, Caro Janse, Bezuidenhout, Carli, Matthee, Marianne, and Stolzenburg, Victor. 2020. *Globalization and gender inequality: Evidence from South Africa*. South Africa: UNU-WIDER. https://doi.org/10.35188/UNU-WIDER/2020/854-2

Wei, Ming. 2016. Language ideology and identity seeking: Perceptions of college learners of English in China. *Journal of Language, Identity & Education* 15 (2): 100–113. https://doi.org/10.1080/15348458.2015.1137477.

Wu, Manfred Man-fat. 2018. Is second language teaching enslavement or empowerment? Insights from an Hegelian perspective. *Educational Philosophy and Theory* 50 (1): 39–48. https://doi.org/10.1080/00131857.2017.1317626.

Wu, Manfred Man-fat. 2020. Second language teaching for global citizenship. *Globalisation, Societies and Education* 18 (3): 330–342. https://doi.org/10.1080/14767724.2019.1693349.

Wu, Manfred Man-fat. 2023. *Sublating second language research and practices: Contribution from the Hegelian perspective*. London: Routledge. https://doi.org/10.4324/9781003372240.

Wu, Manfred Man-fat. 2024. Missing links in L2 teaching approaches in the context of globalisation. In *Progress in Education*, vol. 78, ed. Robert V. Nata, 69–94. New York: Nova Science.

Wu, Manfred Man-fat, Römhild, Ricardo, and Nishizaki, Mona. In press. Teaching English as an international language for global citizenship. In Nicola Galloway and Ali Fuad Selvi (eds.) *The Routledge handbook of English as an international language*. Routledge.

CHAPTER 5

L2 Autonomy for Multilingualism

Abstract Second language (L2) autonomy is an integral part of L2 identity. The radical and large-scale contextual changes for L2 learning globalisation have brought an increasing multilingualism resulting in an emerging need to reconceptualise L2 autonomy, a notion coined in the 1980s. This chapter aims to meet this requirement by harnessing L2 autonomy with Hegelian philosophy. From a Hegelian perspective, L2 autonomy is dynamic, dialectical in development involving contradictions and struggles, intimately related to morality and politics, and relies heavily on learners' awareness of their surroundings and mutual recognition with others. L2 autonomy not only facilitates L2 learning but also performs political and moral functions, and enables learners to achieve freedom. The above features make the Hegelian perspective highly relevant for updating the conceptualisation of L2 autonomy in the context of globalisation. How L2 autonomy is related to the larger social environment beyond L2 learning should also be one of the goals for the implementation of L2 autonomy. Finally, because of the interpersonal, social, political, moral, and culture-specific nature of L2 autonomy, a negotiated approach is recommended for the nurturing of L2 autonomy.

Keywords Ethical life (*Sittlichkeit*) · Hegel · L2 autonomy · Democracy · Mutual recognition · Negotiated approach

© The Author(s), under exclusive license to Springer Nature Switzerland AG 2024
M. M. Wu, *Globalisation and Second Language Identity*,
https://doi.org/10.1007/978-3-031-68248-3_5

INTRODUCTION

The term learner autonomy was first coined by Holec, who defined it as "the ability to take charge of one's own learning" (Holec 1981: 3). When it was first proposed in the 80s, learner autonomy was a general concept not attached to any academic discipline. With the increasing amount of research over time, learner autonomy has become popular in many disciplines, and this concept has been extended to embrace psychology in the learning process and learning content (Little 1991), responsibility (Dickinson 1994), and right (Benson 2000). As in many research areas, learner autonomy has developed into a sub-field in L2 research. A traditional view is that L2 autonomy is intimately related to control (Lenkaitis 2020), and according to this view an autonomous L2 learner is able to control the psychological and socio-cultural dimensions that are related to his L2 learning. The dimensions for control include cognition, reflection, metacognitive knowledge, self-management, motivation, anxiety, beliefs, and preferences. The control of these dimensions constitutes effective L2 learning. Reference can be made to Raya and Vieira (1995) for a detailed historical review of the development of L2 autonomy in L2 learning.

A recent trend in the shift in focus from the individualistic and cognitive approach to a social-interactionist one in L2 autonomy research identified interactions with others as a possible origin of L2 autonomy (see Wu 2024). The transition from the behaviouristic and communicative approaches to an integrative approach in computer-assisted language learning illustrates this trend of the social construction of reality and knowledge (Gimeno-Sanz 2016). However, even if proposals on the social focus of L2 autonomy research are found among L2 researchers, references are only made on the interpersonal level. The overly individualistic conceptualisation of autonomy not only in L2 research but also in philosophical discussions has been criticised over time (see Nickel 2007). This is especially true in recent decades with globalisation causing increasing interdependence among individuals (Illés 2012; Méndez 2018). However, little attention has been given to the struggles involved in L2 autonomy and how L2 learning is related to the larger social environment, in which globalisation plays an important part. With increasing globalisation and multilingualism, the individualistic conceptualisation of autonomy proposed by Holec (1981) is no longer adequate for understanding, analysing, and researching L2 autonomy (Benson and Lamb 2020).

L2 learning constitutes an integral part of multilingualism, especially in the present-day increasing internationalisation of universities on a global scale (Doiz et al. 2013; Gao and Zheng 2019; Wu in press). L2 autonomy is undoubtedly a major contributor to successful L2 learning, as it has been found to be positively related to learning outcomes (Lenkaitis 2020). According to Little et al. (2017), language is the means for learners to control and shape all aspects of their learning. However, despite the intimate relationships between these two notions and the call for research on L2 autonomy and multilingualism by Godwin-Jones (2011) more than a decade ago, research focusing on these two areas to date has been scant. Benson and Lamb (2020) discuss how the "multilingual turn" in applied linguistics places the demand for a conceptual shift on autonomy from the original definition coined by Holec (1981) to embrace multilingualism and the digital world. Given the exponential increase in exposure to foreign languages thanks to the rapid development in digital communication technology, L2 learners are given more choices (a fundamental element of learner autonomy) in terms of the languages they can select for learning. Another issue is that multilingualism does not imply full competence in different languages, and this creates uncertainties regarding the aims of formal language education (e.g., the competence standard for globally recognised qualifications) unquestioned by educators for years (Benson and Lamb 2020).

The ubiquity of out-of-class informal learning made available by communication technologies results in the blurring boundary between classroom and out-of-class language learning (Reinders 2020). Benson and Lamb (2020) propose a shift in focus from taking charge of one's L2 learning to making informed choices about the contexts of language use. In multilingualism, there is a fluid relationship between learners and the languages they learn, particularly in emerging contexts, and more negotiation in real-life contexts with using English as an international language is required (Illés 2012). The lack of exposure to English has now been replaced by too much exposure, therefore pedagogical issues such as how to spend classroom time and the time for take-home assignments have emerged. Given these changes, Illés (2012) advocates for learner's capacity of independent thinking and action (especially in the international setting) as the core element for autonomy.

Another possible conceptual change required for L2 autonomy is learners' awareness of learning resources instead of taking control of their own learning (Kashiwa and Benson 2018). This is highly consistent with

Illés's (2012) proposal of learner responsibility for the selection of classroom tasks and materials. Finally, the two features of L2 autonomy in the context of multilingualism Benson and Lamb (2020) suggest are that it is "a dynamic, situated construct, afforded or constrained by forces within the broader context in which learning is occurring" (84) (which shares similarities with the post-structuralist approaches to L2 identity) and "the need to learn how to learn from using the language in multilingual contexts" (84). As will be introduced in greater detail in the next section, the anthropological and social nature of Hegel's (1953, 1977) philosophy makes it pertinent for generating insights for new conceptualisations of L2 autonomy in the context of multilingualism. An example is that Hegel's (1977) view of self as dynamic, fluid, and in constant mutual influences with the outer social environment is highly in tune with the multilingual language learning autonomy introduced by Benson and Lamb (2020) and Illés (2012).

The aim of this chapter is to align L2 autonomy with a Hegelian perspective to overcome the inadequacy of the original conceptualisation of learner autonomy. The dialectical method Hegel (1969, 1977) employed to analyse the different developmental stages of consciousness involves negation, and the synthesis between the positive and negative. This implies that there are struggles and contradictions in the transition from one stage (or "moment" in Hegel's term) to another (Wu 2018, 2024). The dialectic method of the Hegelian perspective enables an alternative view on L2 autonomy: Its development involves a series of struggles, from the intra-individual level both cognitively and psychologically, the classroom level involving fellow students and teachers, the institutional level involving school and national policies, and finally to the societal level involving the commercial world, virtual world and culture (Rivers 2015). Struggles on these levels are increasingly transparent in the multilingual and multicultural world. The dialectic method of Hegel echoes the non-linear development, maintenance and implementation of L2 autonomy documented (Godwin-Jones 2019).

An outline of this chapter is as follows. In the next section, ideas from the Hegelian perspective which are relevant to L2 autonomy are introduced. How research findings and discussions on L2 autonomy in the multilingual context to date can be informed by the Hegelian perspective are introduced in the third section. Discussions in this part are made on three levels, the intra-individual level, the interpersonal level, and the collective level. The account on the individual level will focus on how L2 autonomy is dialectically developed within an individual in the context of multilingualism. Details on the process involved in mutual recognition, which takes place interpersonally and contributes to the development of L2 autonomy, are given in the account on the interpersonal level. Finally, how the larger contexts such as culture, politics, and morality are related to L2 autonomy, again, in the multilingual context, will be explored.

A Hegelian Account of Autonomy

In Hegel's theories of language, language has the special function of transforming images into signs, and the use of signs allows individuals to externalise their subjective meanings (Hegel 1971). As labour, language is a middle term for the manifestation of individuals' inner subjectivities. This enables mutual recognition to occur and consciousness at both the individual and collective levels to progress to higher stages of development. The use of language negates and annihilates the object, achieves objectivity, overcomes consciousness's alienation from the world, and allows individuals to come to terms with the world through a dialectical process (Surber 2011). In the words of Surber, a contemporary scholar on Hegelian philosophy of language, the objectifying function (transforming inner subjective ideas into objective reality) of language allows individuals to emerge and define themselves. Language plays an important role in the achievement of L2 autonomy, and is an impetus in transforming "*individual-in-itself*" to "*individual-for-itself*". An implication is that L2 learning can foster L2 autonomy, and a higher level of L2 autonomy in turn fosters better L2 learning. The existence of this mutually reinforcing relationship between L2 autonomy and L2 learning also implies that L2 autonomy has an important role to play in L2 learning.

Hegel did not discuss autonomy in L2 learning explicitly. However, his views on how mutual recognition contributes to the development of self and autonomy in the political and moral sense in civil society shed light on his views on L2 autonomy. Hegel states that the relationship formed by mutual recognition "forms the substance of ethical life, namely, of the family, of sexual love (there this unity has the form of particularity), of patriotism ... of love towards God, of bravery too, ... also of honour ..." (Hegel 1971: 177). However, instead of being a smooth process, the discovery of self involves contradictions of one's view of self as a pure subject and therefore involves struggles. This self-knowing sense also allows individuals to know how their own selves are related to the legal and moral aspects of society. Mutual recognition is the key to the development of the identity of individuals, in which autonomy is an integral part. Hegel expresses that "(t)his unity of being-for-another or making oneself a Thing, and of being-for-self, this universal substance, speaks its universal language in the customs and laws of its nation" (Hegel 1977: 213). In pointing out an individual's realisation into a member of civil society, Hegel also states that

> the disposition to make oneself a member of one of the moments of civil society by one's own act, through one's energy, industry, and skill, to maintain oneself in this position, and to fend for oneself only through this process of mediating oneself with the universal, while in this way gaining recognition both in one's own eyes and in the eyes of others (Hegel 1975: 131).

Hegel holds a communitarian view of morality, and this view has been extended to his treatment of autonomy (Stern 1989). Stern (1989) provides details on how Hegel's theories on ethical life (*Sittlichkeit*) can preserve rational autonomy. According to him (Stern 1989), autonomy in the general sense is a social enterprise, and Hegel divides the ethical life (*Sittlichkeit*) into three self-contained spheres: family, civil society, and state. Individuals in a family which emphasises love and unity are unreflective and subjective, and therefore the family provides limited space for individuals to realise their freedom. Civil society is the location where individuals can pursue their concepts of the good. Finally, the state functions as a mechanism to preserve the structure of civil society to maintain its stability. In Hegel's view, an autonomous person in the political sense is a law-abiding and responsible member of civil society (Stern 1989). Hoffman (2014) adds that Hegel "extends the idea of autonomy from the sphere of subjective morality to the horizon of spirit" (256), and ethical life (*Sittlichkeit*) actualises freedom hence social autonomy.

There is a long tradition in philosophy of treating autonomy as intimately related to political life and freedom of individuals. Nickel (2007) offers a historical sketch of how autonomy has been conceptualised among philosophers. According to him, Kerr (2002) is dissatisfied with the earlier exposition of autonomy and adds a moral dimension to it, as how to live with others harmoniously and be morally responsible for the community are important features of autonomy. As described in Chapter 3 of this book, autonomy in the political sense enables individuals to overcome the challenge of the demise of traditional authority, one of the outcomes of globalisation. Individuals are influenced by social norms and their obligations to others, and therefore autonomy is in no way unaffected by social contexts. The above accounts show traces of Hegel's view that autonomy is intimately related to morality with a strong social hue can be found among many philosophers (see Wu 2024).

In the next section, how research and practice in L2 autonomy can be informed by the Hegelian ideas on autonomy, which are morally and politically nuanced, will be explored.

L2 Autonomy for the Multilingual Context

The Multi-Faceted Nature of L2 Autonomy (Intra-Individual Level)

Benson and Voller (1997), pioneers in the study of L2 autonomy, summarised the five senses in which the concept of autonomy has been used in L2 learning. They are learners studying on their own, a set of skills used in self-directed learning, an inborn capacity suppressed by institutional education, learners' responsibility for their own learning, and learners' right to determine their own learning directions. The inborn nature of autonomy is shared by Suliman (2022), who argues that not providing conditions for learners to exercise their autonomy is a suppression of their natural predisposition. The fourth sense, which focuses on self-responsibility, is the closest to Holec's (1981) seminal conceptualisation and embraces the other four senses. This sense resonates highly with Hegel's theories of autonomy, especially in the political sense. L2 autonomy is a significant constituent of individual consciousness, which must be unfolded and realised from abstract rights into concrete rights and duties (Hegel 1953, 1977). This view resonates with the fourth and the last sense in Benson and Voller's (1997) conceptualisation.

Like Hegel (1970), L2 researchers hold the view that L2 learning can raise individuals' consciousness of language and meaning, thus contributing to intellectual development (see Wu 2024). Foreign languages provide learners with windows into the world, which can indirectly contribute to moral and political developments through increased awareness of the social surroundings. The enhanced intellectual capacity of learners raises learners' awareness (Wu 2018, 2021), and contributes to learner autonomy on the intra-individual level. It is because one important criterion for learner autonomy is the awareness of the reasons and responsibilities for learning by learners themselves.

In addition to research on specific language aspects (e.g., Moyer 2017 on phonology), research on L2 autonomy has extended outside classrooms such as self-access centres, computer-aided language learning, distance learning, study abroad, out-of-class learning, and self-instructions (Benson and Lamb 2020). This shows that contemporary L2 researchers have a wider recognition that autonomy exists in different parts of life and society rather than in the L2 classroom only. A relatively neglected aspect is that autonomy has its roots in the concept of democracy and globalisation, which place demands on individuals to be responsible for their own actions (Benson and Lamb 2020). Little et al. (2017) discuss L2 autonomy in relation to plurilingualism, which is nuanced with intercultural competence, democratic citizenship, and language education policy. These two issues echo Hegel's (1953) stance on the political nature of autonomy, and they are intimately related to multilingualism (Angelo 2021; Tlale 2021).

Recognition and L2 Autonomy in the Multilingual Context (Interpersonal Level)

In Hegel's (e.g., 1977) view, the self is constantly in creation through interacting with others and is always in becoming (Bykova 2009). In Hegel's philosophy, the self does not pre-exist but emerges from constant active interactions with others, and language is the chief means for social interactions involving intersubjectivity, or shared meanings among members of a community. In short, language is a carrier of meanings for the construction of identity.

Davis (2022) found close relationships between autonomy with relatedness and interdependence to reflect the importance of social interactions in autonomy among L2 researchers. The significance of social relations is becoming more transparent in the multilingual context because of increasing interdependence among individuals. In many L2 classrooms, a high level of decision-making within a collaborative and supportive environment is provided in the classroom-based approaches aiming at fostering autonomous L2 learning (Little 2009). These social approaches share similarities with Hegel's communitarian perspective and the notion of mutual recognition.

Hegel predicted the emergence of the social constructivist view (as represented by Vygotsky), which states that our subjective meanings are co-constructed and are constantly in the process of reconstruction through our continuous interactions with others (Vygotsky 1978). After going through continuous internal struggles in interacting with others (not only with fellow students but also with teachers), L2 learners develop their autonomy. What also needs to be pointed out is that the key role played by social interactions is highly consistent with the "social turn" in the theory of L2 autonomy (Dörnyei and Ushioda 2011). Applying Hegel's idea of mutual recognition to multilingualism means that L2 learners need to recognise the multiple linguistic and cultural contexts of other speakers and be sensitive to them to achieve mutual recognition for consciousness to progress to the next higher stages of development. As suggested by Illés (2012), there is a need for a reconceptualisation of the notion of learner autonomy to prepare learners for their language use in international contexts.

The process of recognition in Hegel's philosophy is characterised by struggles (e.g., Hegel 1977). Jurist (1987) provides four senses of recognition: cognition, experience, self-knowing, and tragic. All four senses involve struggles both at the intrapersonal level and in relation to others. In the cognitive sense, an individual engages in self-reflection and gains knowledge of himself through confronting another consciousness. Uncertainties and anxiety arise in confronting another consciousness, and the individual involved may experience a loss of self. In the second sense of experience, an individual revises his knowledge of himself with more experiences through interacting with others. In self-knowing, an individual knows that his self is socially constituted. The discovery of self involves contradiction of one's view of self as a pure subject and therefore involves struggles. This self-knowing sense also enables individuals to know how their own self is related to the legal and moral aspects of society. The tragic sense originates in Aristotle's views on Greek tragedy that recognition in Greek tragedy is defined as a bond of love to hate or from hate to love, which shows the struggles involved. All except the last sense are intimately related to L2 autonomy and involve the use of language. Firstly, cognition involves the use of language, self-monitoring, and self-regulation, which are core elements of L2 autonomy. Secondly, experience provides opportunities not only for recognition to take place but also space for L2 autonomy to be developed and implemented, as practising L2 autonomy involves the use of language. Finally, self-knowing is a key constituent of

L2 autonomy, without adequate knowledge of one's beliefs, ability, right, and duty, an individual can hardly achieve autonomy.

Lawrence (2020) recommends a negotiated approach to autonomous L2 learning which emphasises learner independence and learner responsibility in the L2 classroom. In this approach, teachers negotiate with both learners and external authorities about the curriculum, classroom activities, and self-access learning activities. Taking into consideration the changing contexts caused by multilingualism and globalisation, Illés (2012) proposes including negotiation as an element for L2 autonomy. As stated by Illés (2012),

> [c]hanges in the use of English and the subsequent focus on communication processes imply that learner autonomy should include the ability to cope with the linguistic and schematic diversity, the fluidity, and the increased demand for negotiation that interaction in international contexts of use presents. The aim therefore should be to become competent language users who can successfully cope with the demands of real-life communication under their own initiative. The amended definition should thus expand the scope of autonomy and include the ability to manage and control language use, which should, in return, affect the learning process (509).

Lawrence (2020) comments that a negotiated approach is particularly useful for teachers to meet the demands of dynamic, digital, intercultural, and transnational learning environments. Negotiation of curriculum between students and teachers has the same effects as a process syllabus that learner participation and decision-making are fully realised. The emphasis of negotiation of meaning concurs with Hegel's theories of language, in which subjective meanings of individuals and intersubjectivity play critical roles in the development of consciousness. However, teachers trained in the expository mode may exhibit resistance and difficulties in implementing negotiation. Learners who are children and adolescents engaging in full-time institutional schooling may be too used to teacher-led instruction and exhibit resistance to this type of autonomous L2 learning.

Contrary to common belief, interdependence instead of independence is one of the goals of learner autonomy (Davis 2022). Little and his colleagues made the same remark that feeling connected with others is a prominent element of autonomy (Little 2022). Again, the Hegelian perspective (e.g., in terms of mutual recognition, ethical life (*Sittlichkeit*) and morality) offers a pertinent alternative for extending the concept of L2 autonomy,

Culture, Context, and L2 Autonomy (Collective Level)

In learning foreign languages, learners inevitably experience struggles due to cultural differences (Wu 2024). Hegel's theories on language treat L2 learning as facilitative to the exchanges of different "shapes of consciousness", and involves culture learning. However, in the process of foreign culture learning, in the same vein of an individual interacting with another, an individual will experience a sense of loss, estrangement, and struggles before attaining a more general and universal perspective as suggested by Hegel's dialectical perspective. Like Ridley (2003), Schmenk (2005) is of the view that examining the role of autonomy in L2 research involves reflections (a key element in Hegelian mutual recognition) on political and cultural concerns, and these issues have been under-represented in research to date. Godwin-Jones (2019) shares a similar view, that school and national cultures influence the development of L2 autonomy. It is only by taking more seriously the cultural backdrop of the Western traditions of autonomy that L2 autonomy can be applicable to different cultural contexts. However, Lin and Reinders (2019) argue that culture may not be as important as an influence on L2 autonomy as previously suggested. In this part, how context and culture contribute to the struggles for autonomy will be discussed with the aim of generating some possible solutions to these two contradictory views.

The process of enculturation takes place within a specific cultural order, and therefore L2 autonomy is culture-specific (Godwin-Jones 2019). In their study on the intrusion of cultural identity of L2 learners, Soruç and Griffiths (2015) remark that cultural identity is a mirror that reflects the ideological battle and the underlying dynamics of the struggles of individuals. L2 learning is a process of a mélange of local culture and culture of the target language. For multilingual learners, this process is even more complicated as multiple languages (thus cultures) are involved. The cultural resistance of learners documented (see Xing and Turner 2020) to date is a manifestation of the struggles for autonomy, as L2 learning contributes to the formation of self-identity and autonomy. Zheng (2013) identified clashes in the Chinese learners' self-image and the native speaker norms of English-speaking countries. In her study, she found that Chinese learners constructed their ideal and ought-to self based on the English native speaker norm in their English learning. However, given their self-image being nuanced with Chinese culture, it was found that many of these norms are unrealistic and unattainable. Kohn (2018) calls for the emancipation of learners from native speaker identity of the English language and become "speakers of English in their own right" (1). Given this background, a negotiated pedagogical approach, again, is required for cultural differences. These issues deserve more attention by researchers in multilingualism.

There are four types of culture that can influence autonomy: Educational and academic cultures, professional language teaching cultures, organisational cultures of educational institutes, and cultures of social class and gender (Palfreyman 2003). Learner beliefs are liable to change due to the influences of context and belief changes in turn can result in changes in context (Benson et al. 2003). Adopting a critical perspective, Pennycook (1997) is of the view that both the achievement of autonomy and culture learning involve struggles as suggested by the Hegelian dialectic of mutual recognition. His view is that L2 autonomy development inevitably involves culture learning, and it requires learners' awareness of and struggle for cultural alternatives. Voice, a site for struggle, is of particular importance in this process. Alienated learners can develop their "voice" (or subjectivity from the Hegelian perspective) by engaging in the socio-cultural contexts which they are in (Lamb 2000). Thus, cultural differences exist in L2 autonomy, and cultural variations in L2 autonomy are an important future research area (Gremmo and Riley 1995), especially under the context of multilingualism and globalisation. Illés's (2012) conclusion is that Holec's (1981) original conceptualisation of autonomy which focuses only on the individual level is inadequate, given the broad coverage of the concept of autonomy and changing circumstances.

Culturism is an issue in learner autonomy that deserves attention. Holliday (2003), a pioneer in the L2 research field, delineates three approaches to autonomy, namely, native speakerist, cultural relativist, and social autonomy, and provides examples of research on learner autonomy that is heavily nuanced with the native speakerist approach. With native speakerism as a hegemony, the Western-culture-based perspective should be avoided (Toh 2016). Two alternative approaches, cultural relativism, and social autonomy, aim to develop special methodologies on learner autonomy. These two methodologies suit other cultures and encourage L2 educators to cease to be culturists, and should be adopted. This suggestion is highly applicable to L2 learning in multilingual and globalised contexts. The concept of autonomy is central to European liberal-democratic and liberal-humanist thought, which is based on the Enlightenment concept of rationality at the individual level (Pennycook 1997). Therefore, the concept of autonomy may be valued differently in other cultural contexts. Kálmán (2019), on the contrary, comments that the concept of autonomy is far from being a Western one and is equally applicable to Asian students. However, due to cultural differences, Asian L2 learners may need special attention on some of their cultural characteristics such as being more collectivistic and possessing a stronger sense of social hierarchy between them and teachers than Westerners do (Loh and Ang 2020).

Because of the intricate relationship between autonomy and culture, Pennycook (1997) proposes using culturally responsive teaching methods for the development of learner autonomy and raising cultural awareness for the promotion of learner autonomy as a universal concept. This proposal has been echoed by researchers such as Tan et al. (2021) and Yasin (2023). Little (2022) as well as Little et al. (2017), while viewing autonomy as a universal concept for human beings, acknowledges that cultural differences exist in the conceptualisation of autonomy. These differences exist both between cultures and within cultures, and children socialised in one social knowledge system may have difficulties adapting to teaching devised in another culture. Therefore, educators, including those involved in L2 teaching, must pay special attention when developing pedagogies for the development of L2 autonomy.

Literature to date seems to show that culture exerts significant influences on L2 autonomy, which is contrary to the view of Lin and Reinders (2019). It is possible that some elements of L2 autonomy are universally shared by individuals of different cultures, while some elements are culture-specific as indicated by research findings to date.

CONCLUSION: TEACHER TRAINING
AS THE STARTING POINT

Discussions that have been undertaken in this chapter have indicated that a Hegelian extension of L2 autonomy is a promising direction for the reconceptualisation of L2 autonomy for the needs of increasing speed and extent of globalisation and multilingualism. Given that discussions and research on this topic are a relatively new area, teacher training is recommended as the priority for future endeavours. Details are given in the remainder of this section.

To date, discussions on the moral and political aspects of L2 autonomy highlighted in this chapter have not been common. Correspondingly, there are lacunae in this area of teacher training. Strengthening teachers' competence on fostering L2 autonomy and cultivation of their positive attitudes towards enhancing L2 autonomy are essential. This is especially true given the powerful influences of teacher identity (which is formed partly by teacher autonomy) on many aspects of L2 learner characteristics and learning outcomes to be described in the next chapter.

Vázquez (2020) emphasises the importance of teacher autonomy in fostering L2 autonomy of learners. However, he argues that there has been a severe lack of research on the effectiveness of a teacher-based approach for the enhancement of L2 autonomy. His conclusion is that despite being a valid concept, L2 autonomy needs more empirical support and action research, which relies heavily on teachers, is an effective means for the empirical basis of the concept.

Both the Hegelian perspective and past research on L2 learning have indicated that there is a positive reciprocal relationship between recognition and L2 autonomy (e.g., Wu 2024). Recognition is also a powerful motivator for L2 learning, as motivation is part of learner autonomy and self-identity. Therefore, teachers should have knowledge of the relationships between different variables and make the best use of these relationships to result in the effective nurturing of learners' L2 autonomy. A specific example is that opportunities for interactions between learners and between learners and teachers should be provided to the largest extent in the L2 classroom because negotiation is an effective means for achieving mutual recognition (thus L2 autonomy) as suggested in this chapter. Guidelines on the use of negotiation in L2 teaching in the primary, secondary, and tertiary education levels as well as in teacher education have been available for more than two decades (Breen and

Littlejohn 2000). Some examples of the focuses for negotiation, to name a few, are assessment, project work, and syllabuses.

Reflection is an effective means for raising the self-awareness of learners in their process of struggles in their L2 learning, and teachers play an important role in facilitating reflection of learners in the L2 classroom (Baker and Feng 2022; Feng and Kim 2022). This recommendation is popular among educationalists such as Dewey (1938). According to Ridley (2003), the first step teachers need to take is to let learners know that they are the agents of their own learning, and teachers can exert a huge influence in assisting learners in understanding their learning process.

REFERENCES

Angelo, Ria. 2021. Against the multilingual turn as paradigm replacement: Reconsidering Kubota's charge. *Open Linguistics* 7 (1): 111–115. https://doi.org/10.1515/opli-2021-0007.

Baker, Will, and Fan Fang. 2022. Intercultural citizenship and the internationalisation of higher education: The role of English language teaching. *Journal of English as a Lingua Franca* 11 (1): 63–75. https://doi.org/10.1515/jelf-2022-2067.

Benson, Phil. 2000. Autonomy as a learners' and teachers' right. In *Learner autonomy, teacher autonomy: Future directions*, ed. Ian Mcgrath, Barbara Sinclair, and Terry Lamb, 111–117. Harlow: Longman.

Benson, Phil and Lamb, Terry. 2020. Autonomy in the age of multilingualism. In Manuel Jimenez Raya and Flavia Vieira (eds.) *Autonomy in language education: Theory, research and practice*, 74–88. New York and London: Routledge. https://doi.org/10.4324/9780429261336-7

Benson, Phil, and Peter Voller, eds. 1997. *Autonomy and independence in language learning*. London: Longman.

Benson, Phil, Chik, Alice, and Lim Hye-Yeon. 2003. Becoming autonomous in an Asian context: Autonomy as a sociocultural process. In David Palfreyman and Richard C. Smith (eds.) *Learner autonomy across cultures: Language education perspectives*, 23–40. New York: Palgrave Macmillan. https://doi.org/10.1057/9780230504684_2

Breen, Michael P., and Andrew Littlejohn. 2000. Introduction and overview. In *Classroom decision-making: Negotiation and process syllabuses in practice*, ed. Michael P. Breen and Andrew Littlejohn, 1–4. Cambridge: Cambridge University Press.

Bykova, Marina F. 2009. Spirit and concrete subjectivity in Hegel's phenomenology of spirit. In Kenneth R. Westphal (ed.) *The Blackwell guide to Hegel's phenomenology of spirit*, 265–295. Chichester: Wiley-Blackwell. https://doi.org/10.1002/9781444306224.ch13

Davis, William S. 2022. Autonomy, competence, relatedness, and beneficence: Exploring the Interdependence of basic needs satisfaction in postsecondary world language education. *Journal for the Psychology of Language Learning* 4 (1): e415422. https://doi.org/10.52598/jpll/4/1/2

Dewey, John. 1938. *Experience and education*. New York: Collier Books.

Dickinson, Leslie. 1994. Preparing learners: Toolkit requirements for preparing/ orienting learners. In *Self-access and the adult language learner*, ed. Edith Esch, 39–49. London: CILT.

Doiz, Aintzane, Lasagabaster David, and Juan Sierra. 2013. Globalisation, internationalisation, multilingualism and linguistic strains in higher education. *Studies in Higher Education* 38 (9): 1407–1421. https://doi.org/10.1080/03075079.2011.642349.

Dörnyei, Zoltán and Ushioda, Ema. 2011. *Teaching and researching motivation*. 2nd edn. Harlow: Pearson Education. https://doi.org/10.4324/9781315833750

Feng, Maomao, and Hoe Kyeung Kim. 2022. EFL Teachers' spatial construction of linguistic identities for sustainable development in globalization. *Sustainability* 14: 4532. https://doi.org/10.3390/su14084532.

Gao, Xuesong, and Yongyan Zheng. 2019. Multilingualism and higher education in Greater China. *Journal of Multilingual and Multicultural Development* 40 (7): 555–561. https://doi.org/10.1080/01434632.2019.1571073.

Gimeno-Sanz, Ana. 2016. Moving a step further from "Integrative CALL". What's to come? *Computer Assisted Language Learning* 29 (6): 1102–1115. https://doi.org/10.1080/09588221.2015.1103271

Godwin-Jones, Robert. 2011. Autonomous language learning. *Language Learning & Technology* 15 (3): 4–11. https://doi.org/10.1002/9781405198431.wbeal0365.

Godwin-Jones, Robert. 2019. Riding the digital wilds: Learner autonomy and informal language learning. *Language Learning & Technology* 23 (1): 8–25. https://doi.org/10.10125/44667

Gremmo, Marie-José., and Philip Riley. 1995. Autonomy, self-direction and self-access in language teaching and learning: The history of an idea. *System* 23 (2): 151–164. https://doi.org/10.1016/0346-251X(95)00002-2.

Hegel, Georg Wilhelm Friedrich. 1953. *The philosophy of right*. Translated by Thomas Malcolm Knox. Oxford: Oxford University Press.

Hegel, Georg Wilhelm Friedrich. 1970. *Werke*. Edited by Eva Moldenhauer and Karl Markus. Frankfurt: Suhrkamp.

Hegel, Georg Wilhelm Friedrich. 1971. *Philosophy of mind: Being part three of the encyclopaedia of philosophical sciences*. Translated by William Wallace. Oxford: Clarendon Press.

Hegel, Georg Wilhelm Friedrich. 1977. *Phenomenology of spirit*. Translated by Arnold Vincent Miller. Oxford: Oxford University Press.

Hoffma, Christian. 2014. Autonomy and the concrete universal. Moral subjectivity and its function in Hegel's philosophy of right. *Hegel Bulletin* 35 (2): 252–272. https://doi.org/10.1017/hgl.2014.29

Holec, Henri. 1981. *Autonomy in foreign language learning*. Strasbourg: Council of Europe.

Holliday, Adrian. 2003. Social autonomy: Addressing the dangers of culturism in TESOL. In David Palfreyman and Robert C. Smith (eds.) *Learner autonomy across cultures: Language education perspectives*, 110–126. New York: Palgrave Macmillan. https://doi.org/10.1057/9780230504684_7

Illés, Éva. 2012. Learner autonomy revisited. *ELT Journal* 66 (4): 505–513. https://doi.org/10.1093/elt/ccs044.

Jurist, Elliot L. 1987. Hegel's concept of recognition. *The Owl of Minerva* 19 (1): 5–22. https://doi.org/10.5840/owl198719132.

Kálmán, Csaba. 2019. Human resource policy makers', teachers', and adult learners' views on the impact of context- and teacher-generated autonomy on adult learners' L2 motivation: Interview studies in Hungarian corporate contexts. *Journal of Adult Learning, Knowledge and Innovation* 3 (2): 49–60. https://doi.org/10.1556/2059.03.2019.08.

Kashiwa, Mayumi, and Phil Benson. 2018. A road and a forest: Conceptions of the relationship between in-class and out-of-class learning at home and abroad. *TESOL Quarterly* 52 (4): 725–747. https://doi.org/10.1002/tesq.409.

Kerr, Donald. 2002. Devoid of community: Examining conceptions of autonomy in education. *Educational Theory* 52 (1): 13–25. https://doi.org/10.1111/j.1741-5446.2002.00013.x.

Kohn, Kurt. 2018. MY English: A social constructive perspective on ELF. *Journal of English as a Lingua Franca* 7 (1): 1–24. https://doi.org/10.1515/jelf-2018-0001.

Lamb, Terry. 2000. Finding a voice: Learner autonomy and teacher education in an urban context. In *Learner autonomy, teacher autonomy: Future directions*, ed. Barbara Sinclair, Ian McGrath, and Terry Lamb, 118–137. Harlow: Longman.

Lawrence, Geoff. 2020. A pedagogical framework to support teachers in today's dynamic, digital, intercultural, and transnational learning environments. In Osman Z. Barnawi and Anwar Ahmed (eds.) *TESOL teacher education in a transnational world: Turning challenges into innovative prospects*, 121–138.

London and New York: Routledge. https://doi.org/10.4324/978100300 8668

Lenkaitis, Chesla Ann. 2020. Technology as a mediating tool: Videoconferencing, L2 learning, and learner autonomy. *Computer Assisted Language Learning* 33 (5–6): 483–509. https://doi.org/10.1080/09588221.2019. 1572018.

Lin, Lilan, and Hayo Reinders. 2019. Students' and teachers' readiness for autonomy: Beliefs and practices in developing autonomy in the Chinese context. *Asia Pacific Education Review* 20: 69–89. https://doi.org/10. 1007/s12564-018-9564-3.

Little, David. 1991. *Learner autonomy: 1: Definitions, issues and problems*. Dublin: Authentik.

Little, David. 2009. Language learner autonomy and the European language portfolio: Two L2 English examples. *Language Teaching* 42 (2): 222–233. https://doi.org/10.1017/S0261444808005636.

Little, David. 2022. Language learner autonomy: Rethinking language teaching. *Language Teaching* 55: 64–73. https://doi.org/10.1017/S02614448200 00488.

Little, David., Dam, Leni, and Legenhausen, Lienhard. (2017). *Language learner autonomy: Theory, practice and research*. Bristol, Blue Ridge Summit: Multilingual Matters. https://doi.org/10.21832/LITTLE8590

Loh, Raymond Chee-Yen and Ang, Chin-Siang. 2020. Unravelling cooperative learning in higher education. *Research in Social Sciences and Technology* 5 (2): 22–39. https://doi.org/10.46303/ressat.05.02.2

Méndez, Alberto Ruiz. 2018. Who are the subjects of justice in a globalized world? From the 'unidimensional identity' to the 'diversity of identities'. In Concha Roldán, Daniel Brauer, and Johannes Rohbeck (eds.) *Philosophy of globalization*, 153–166. Berlin and Boston: Walter de Gruyter. https://doi. org/10.1515/9783110492415-012

Moyer, Alene. 2017. Autonomy in second language phonology: Choice vs. limits. *Language Teaching* 50 (3): 395–411. https://doi.org/10.1017/S02614448 15000191

Nickel, Jodi. 2007. Interests and purposes in conceptions of autonomy. *Paideusis: Journal of the Canadian Philosophy of Education Society* 16 (1): 29–40. https://doi.org/10.7202/1072604ar

Palfreyman, David. 2003. Introduction: Culture and learner autonomy. In David Palfreyman and Robert C. Smith (eds.) *Learner autonomy across cultures: Language education perspectives*, 1–19. New York: Palgrave Macmillan. https://doi.org/10.1057/9780230504684_1

Pennycook, Alastair. 1997. Cultural alternatives and autonomy. In Phil Benson and Peter Voller (eds.) *Autonomy and independence in language learning*, 35–53. London: Longman. https://doi.org/10.4324/9781315842172-4

Reinders, Hayo. 2020. A framework for learning beyond the classroom. In Manuel Jimenez Raya and Flavia Vieira (eds.) *Autonomy in language education: Theory, research and practice*, 63–73. New York and London: Routledge. https://doi.org/10.4324/9780429261336-6

Ridley, Jennifer. 2003. Learners' ability to reflect on language and on their learning. In David Little, Jennifer Ridley, and Ema Ushioda (eds.) *Learner autonomy in the foreign language classroom: Teacher, learner, curriculum and assessment*, 78–89. Dublin: Authentik.

Rivers, Damian J. 2015. The authorities of autonomy and English-only: Serving whose interests? In Daiman J. Rivers (ed.) *Resistance to the known: Counter-conduct in language education*, 94–118. Houndmills: Palgrave Macmillan. https://doi.org/10.1057/9781137345196_5

Schmenk, Barbara. 2005. Globalizing learner autonomy. *TESOL Quarterly* 39 (1): 107–118. https://doi.org/10.2307/3588454.

Soruç, Adem, and Carol Griffiths. 2015. Identity and the spoken grammar dilemma. *System* 50: 32–42. https://doi.org/10.1016/j.system.2015.03.007.

Stern, Paul. 1989. On the relation between rational autonomy and ethical community: Hegel's critique of Kantian morality. *PRAXIS International* 3: 234–248.

Suliman, Wijdan Mohieldeen Mohammed. 2022. Implications of oral presentation for fostering learners' autonomy: A case study with Saudi learners majoring in English as a foreign language. *Journal of English Teaching* 8 (1): 107–118. https://doi.org/10.33541/jet.v8i1.3293

Surber, Jere O'Neill. 2011. Hegel's philosophy of language: The unwritten volume. In Stephen Houlgate and Michael Baur (eds.) *A companion to Hegel*, 243–262. Chichester, West Sussex and Malden: Wiley-Blackwell. https://doi.org/10.1002/9781444397161.ch11

Tan, Dongyao, Horane A. Diatta-Holgate, and Chantal Levesque-Bristol. 2021. Perceived autonomy supportive and culturally responsive environments contribute to international students' participation and willingness to communicate. *Current Psychology* 42: 7629–7648. https://doi.org/10.1007/s12144-021-02063-1.

Tlale, Lloyd D. N. 2021. Managing and leading multiculturalism and multilingualism in an inclusive school environment. In Tsediso Michael Makoelle, Thabo Makhalemele, and Pierre du Plessis (eds.) *School leadership for democratic education in South Africa: Perspectives, achievements and future challenges post-apartheid*, 116–133. New York: Routledge. https://doi.org/10.4324/9781003121367-8

Toh, Glenn. 2016. Doing justice to an English as a lingua franca paradigm. *Journal of English as a Lingua Franca* 5 (2): 355–367. https://doi.org/10.1515/jelf-2016-0024.

Vázquez, Borja Manzano. 2020. A study into pre-service FL teachers' perceptions of their willingness, ability, and opportunity to promote learner autonomy. In Manuel Jimenez Raya and Flavia Vieira (eds.) *Autonomy in language education: Theory, research and practice*, 191–207. New York and London: Routledge. https://doi.org/10.4324/9780429261336-15

Vygotsky, Lev Semenovich. 1978. *Mind in society: The development of higher psychological processes*. Cambridge: Harvard University Press.

Wu, Manfred Man-fat. 2018. Is second language teaching enslavement or empowerment? Insights from an Hegelian perspective. *Educational Philosophy and Theory* 50 (1): 39–48. https://doi.org/10.1080/00131857.2017.131 7626.

Wu, Manfred Man-fat. 2021. The social nature of second language metacognition. *The Asia Pacific Education Researcher* 31: 499–506. https://doi.org/ 10.1007/s40299-021-00596-4.

Wu, Manfred Man-fat. 2024. *Sublating second language research and practices: Contribution from the Hegelian perspective*. London: Routledge. https://doi. org/10.4324/9781003372240.

Wu, Manfred Man-fat. In press. Harnessing teacher identity for globalisation and internationalisation of TESOL curricula. In Vander Tavares (ed.) *Global and critical perspectives on internationalising TESOL teacher education curricula*. Bristol: Multilingual Matters.

Xing, Fei, and J.E. Turner. 2020. Revisiting Chinese resistance to communicative English: A counter example. *International Journal of Educational Research* 103: 101631. https://doi.org/10.1016/j.ijer.2020.101631.

Yasin, Farra. 2023. The agents of autonomy in decolonising pedagogy: An analysis of autonomy-facilitating approaches to anti-deficit, critical, and culturally responsive education for marginalised women in Ontario, Canada. *Pedagogy, Culture & Society* 31 (4): 793–808. https://doi.org/10.1080/14681366. 2021.1949632.

Zheng, Y. 2013. An inquiry into Chinese learners' English-learning motivational self-images: ENL learner or ELF user? *Journal English as a Lingua Franca* 2 (2): 341–364. https://doi.org/10.1515/jelf-2013-0018.

CHAPTER 6

Globalisation and L2 Teacher Identity

Abstract Globalisation has posed new demands for second language (L2) teachers, necessitating a transformation in their identity to meet the emerging demands in their teaching. This chapter proposes the essential qualities that constitute L2 teacher identity in the context of globalisation. The first quality is awareness and sensitivity towards, knowledge of, and respect for the diversity of Englishes. This is because, with the increasing extent of globalisation and internationalisation of higher education, L2 teachers are encountering learners who are increasingly diverse in terms of native language and culture. A related trait for a globalised L2 teacher identity is a good knowledge of and command over moral education. A strong sense of empathy towards others, especially those who are different from oneself, is another necessary disposition. In terms of ideology, a globalised L2 teacher identity needs to be free from a dichotomous native-speaker/non-native-speaker (NS/NNS) classification to avoid the emergence of "otherness" and marginalisation of learners. The final quality is teachers' commitment to action taking to fulfil their duties to others. L2 teachers engaging in reflection, intercultural activities, local and overseas on-site or virtual service learning projects, and formal training are recommended for the development of the proposed qualities.

© The Author(s), under exclusive license to Springer Nature
Switzerland AG 2024
M. M. Wu, *Globalisation and Second Language Identity*,
https://doi.org/10.1007/978-3-031-68248-3_6

Keywords Globalisation · L2 teacher identity · Intercultural competence · Global citizenship · Morality · Human rights · Duties to others

INTRODUCTION

L2 teacher identity has been consistently found to be related to learners' learning experience and outcomes (e.g., Aboud 2020; Denfeld et al. 2023). Identity is intricately related to personal history, and L2 teachers' identity has been found to change due to the influences of socio-cultural contexts (Mirzaei and Parhizkar 2021). This suggests that L2 teacher identity is highly susceptible to the influences of globalisation. Despite its significance, how L2 teacher identity is affected by globalisation has not been adequately researched. Widodo et al. (2020) lament that although there has been an increasing dearth of research on how L2 teacher identity impacts teaching and learning, attention given to how L2 teacher identity is influenced by the increasing role of English as a global lingua franca and globalisation is far from adequate.

Like learners', L2 teachers' self-identity needs to be transformed to resolve the tensions posed by globalisation as discussed in Chapter 3 of this book. One product of globalisation is the democratisation of English, which is often described as a liberating resource for the masses. The self-identity of L2 teachers needs to be transformed, both for their own adaptation to the globalisation context and for future generations.

Despite research on L2 identity having a long history and having become a convention (see Norton 2021), only recently have L2 researchers paid attention to L2 teacher identity (e.g., Barkhuizen 2017; Karpava 2023; Yazan and Lindahl 2020a). However, the desirable traits of L2 teacher identity for the globalised context have not received due attention from researchers. Among the literature on this area, in a recent handbook on L2 teacher identity (Karpava 2023) how globalisation influences L2 teacher identity is only explored peripherally in some of the chapters in a general manner, together with phenomena such as internationalisation, super diversity, transnationalism, and multilingualism. No references on the traits of L2 teacher identity which are essential for effective teaching in the context of globalisation (i.e., the focus of this chapter) have been made in the book.

Given the above background, this chapter aims to bridge the research gap on the desirable traits for L2 teacher identity for globalisation. The proposed elements to be included in the globalised L2 teacher identity are introduced in the next section. This is followed by recommendations for L2 teacher education and relevant research and theoretical development.

Elements to Be Included in the Globalised L2 Teacher Identity

Awareness and Sensitivity of Diversity

The first quality for a desirable L2 teacher identity for globalisation is an awareness and sensitivity towards the diversity of Englishes. This is because, with the increasing extent of globalisation, L2 teachers will face learners who are increasingly diverse in terms of native language and culture (Moser and Kletzenbauer 2019). A related trait for a globalised L2 teacher identity is a good knowledge of and command over intercultural communications. Sensitivity is required to cater to the needs of a multicultural (and multilingual) classroom to avoid cultural relativism and to provide personalised learning experiences to learners. Intercultural sensitivity (e.g., Kaya et al. 2021) is also an element emphasised in the intercultural service learning model of Rauschert (2023). As will be introduced in the third section of this chapter, service learning is one of the proposed means for L2 teacher education to foster teachers' L2 identity for globalisation. Therefore sensitivity, particularly cultural sensitivity, needs to be included in the L2 teacher training curricula.

Of particular relevance to this aspect is global citizenship (GC). According to UNESCO (2015, 2016), GC is a sense of belonging and membership to the global community and humanity, and engagement in GC means sharing collective responsibility at the global level and taking action to build a better world. Many countries are beginning to be aware of global citizenship education (GCE) in L2 education (Sun and Buripakdi 2023). A conclusion of Davidson and Liu's (2020) analysis of past research on intercultural knowledge is that GC is a central tenet rather than an option in the contemporary globalised context. This implies that GC should be incorporated as a part of globalised L2 teacher identity. Of particular relevance to the focus of this book is the importance of morality in GC. Veuglers (2011) distinguishes moral GC from open GC and socio-political GC, and Schattle (2008, 2009) identified moral cosmopolitanism as an ideology for GC. Oxley and Morris (2013) in their seminal review introduced moral GC as one of the significant GC conceptualisations.

As introduced in the introductory chapter of this book, GCE overlaps with human rights education (Starkey 2023). Two key human rights to be recognised for GCE are cosmopolitan right and hospitality right (Kant 1957), which have been proposed as part of L2 learning for GCE (Wu 2020). Cosmopolitan right is an individual's right to be affiliated with the cosmopolitan federation which is free and voluntary in its establishment, organisation and participation (Kant 1970). Hospitality right, on the other hand, refers to "the right of a stranger not to be treated as an enemy when he arrives in the land of another" (Kant 1957: 20). L2 teacher educators need to possess an awareness and knowledge of how GC is related to human rights.

Knowledge, Skills, and Values for Moral Education

Chapters 3 and 4 of this book call for moral elements for L2 identity because of globalisation's repercussions on L2 identity. A recurrent and overarching theme connecting discussions of this book is that globalisation has given rise to the need for moral education, and L2 teachers should be harnessed with the necessary knowledge, skills, and values for moral education. It has been suggested that the moral tradition (which views teaching as involving moral judgements for viewing the construction of teacher identity) compared to the craft tradition, the scientific tradition, and the artistic tradition can better capture teachers' trajectory in the development of their professional identity (Coldron and Smith 1999). This view concurs with the stance adopted in this book, that there is a strong need for moral elements in globalised L2 teacher identity.

The element of GC proposed to be part of the L2 teacher identity above is also highly related to moral education. As explicated above, GC involves human rights and therefore promoting GCE is at the same time implementing moral education, particularly in terms of global justice, respect for cultural diversity, personhood and humanity, and global harmony (Akkari and Maleq 2020; Li 2022). One conclusion of Sun's (2020) critical analysis of UNESCO's (2015) GCE framework is that learners should respect the rights of others. Echoing De Ruyter and Spiecker (2008), Sun (2020) argues that GCE should involve teaching learners to respect the rights of others and to evaluate the moral qualities of societies. Another remark of Sun (2020) is that successful GCE requires learners to have their identity attached to the global community. Biberman-Shalev (2021) identified the motivational factors for pre-service teachers in Israel for learning and teaching global education. She reports that social justice and a multicultural orientation among knowledge and skills, as well as instrumental benefits, are the strongest motivators for teaching. The above findings indicate the significant roles played by morality in L2 teacher identity in the context of globalisation.

As introduced in Chapter 4, Shani (2003) summarises three approaches to the study of globalised identity, namely, the hyperglobalist, the sceptical and the transformational approaches, which all involve morality. Shani (2003) has also insightfully proposed a shift from political culture basis from territorial states to human rights because of the force of globalisation. While Wu (2020) introduces the inclusion of duties to others as a dimension of global citizenship, Sun (2020) focuses on the importance of the morality UNESCO attributed to the socio-emotional dimension of its GCE conceptual framework. Results of his research with Buripakdi (Sun and Buripakdi 2023) suggest that English teachers have the responsibility to go beyond the linguistic aspect and promote GCE which is highly morality nuanced in their teaching.

A Strong Sense of Empathy

Empathy, which involves emotion, is an integral part of morality (Sun 2020), and emotion has been identified as an important aspect of L2 teacher identity (Badenhorst et al. 2023; Moser and Kletzenbauer 2019; Nazari et al. 2023). Badenhorst et al. (2023) conducted a study on the construction of professional identity among American pre-service teachers participating in a cultural/linguistic immersion programme in Ecuador. Their major finding is that emotion, relationship building, and empathy served as foundational tools for English as a Second Language (ESL) practitioners' cultural responsiveness. GCE introduced in the last section also requires a strong sense of empathy towards others (UNESCO 2021). This is because a key characteristic of a global citizen is the ability to empathise with cultures other than one's own, tolerate differences, and embrace diversity.

Echoing King and Ng (2018), Moser and Kletzenbauer (2019) highlight the need to pay attention to the emotional dimension of L2 teacher identity. They conducted research on how globalisation influences the emotions of English teachers, and findings indicated that being fascinated with English and being influenced by significant others were participants' reasons for selecting English teaching as a profession. The participants stated that globalisation has a positive impact on their continuous professional development, especially through the digitalisation of teaching. Regarding the challenges, participants expressed that they had to deal with complex issues involving the diversity of student backgrounds. Finally, the mediating factors that exerted considerable impacts on participants' teaching styles were pointed out: Administrative tasks such as bureaucracy and regulations, public reputations of teachers, time for reflection, stress, and pressure (Moser and Kletzenbauer 2019).

Abandonment of Native Speaker/Non-native Speaker Classification

In terms of ideology, a globalised L2 teacher identity needs to be free from a dichotomous native speaker/non-native speaker (NS/NNS) classification to avoid the emergence of "otherness" and marginalisation of learners of different native languages and reproduction of social inequalities (Sun and Buripakdi 2021). It has been suggested that globalisation facilitates the power of the West to dominate other parts of the world in terms of democracy, free market, and consumerism (Demuth 2018) by means of cultural standardisation and homogenisation (Kutoba 2018).

Lee and Canagarajah (2019a) as well as Matsumoto (2018) strongly advise L2 educators to move beyond the binary NS/NNS dichotomous classification of English teachers, with the NS perspective pre-dominantly and resiliently rooted in Asia (Houghton 2020; Wang 2020). To overcome the undesirable dichotomous classification, some researchers (Lee and Canagarajah 2019b; Lee and Jenks 2016; You 2016) emphasise the cultivation of a "translingual disposition". According to Lee and Canagarajah (2019a), "translingual disposition" is teachers' "orientation to language diversity, undergirding their performance, shaping their students', as well as their own, experiences in classrooms. We call such disposition to engage with language difference and social diversity, a translingual disposition" (354). It is also "an orientation towards language diversity and difference from a nondeficit perspective—in theorizing language and literacy teacher identity" (352). This call for the deconstruction of the binary perspective is also shared by many L2 researchers such as Baker and Fang (2022), Cross (2020), as well as Feng and Kim (2022). For Cavanagh (2020), the insistence of higher education institutions in promoting native English as the ideal English for internationalisation may be counter-productive to the proposed paradigm shift. These issues should be a focus of reflection among L2 teacher educators. The dichotomous NS/NNS classification tends to create discrimination for NNS teachers, which makes them more prone to psychological distress (Chen et al. 2023).

Translingual disposition can also be understood in terms of critical language awareness (García 2016). Choi (2018), Feng and Kim (2022), as well as Matsumoto (2018) contend that the dichotomous NS/NNS perspective does not allow for the dynamic negotiation of identity, and this will lead to stereotypes and "othering" of individuals (either teachers or students) not being a member of the native-speaking community. Widodo et al. (2020) offer an account of the struggles experienced by Chinese teachers of English in challenging native speakerism in constructing themselves as legitimate English teachers in China. In her study, Matsumoto (2018) identified evidence of negotiation between language teachers and students, and she concludes that a more complex pattern of negotiation happened between teachers and students rather than the simplistic view of teachers possessing more power in the relationship.

Gayton (2016) investigated teachers' perceptions of the global dominance of English on their professional identity. She adopts a theoretical framework that combines the perspectives of school as a community of practice, linguistic imperialism, English as a global language and teacher identity, and found high similarities in Scotland, France and Germany in terms of the following aspects. First, teachers of languages other than English (e.g., French and German) were found to be required to argue more strongly for the importance of the language they taught than those of the English language. Learners of languages other than English were found to be far less motivated than those of English. Finally, teachers of languages other than English expressed doubts about the value of the languages they taught. Language teachers in Gayton's (2016) study in Scotland described their experience of being marginalised and powerless, and parallel trends were found in Scotland, France, and Germany.

An empirical study on the intercultural identity of English teachers in Iran conducted by Tajeddin and Ghaffaryan (2020) shows the dominance of American culture as the representative global culture among participants. The English teachers they researched were also divided in viewing their local culture as a protective wall or limitation in facing globalisation, which indicates the ideological tensions involved. Other struggles (Cooper and Bryan 2020; Fang 2020; Leung and Yip 2020), anti-oppressive pedagogy (Schissel and Stephens 2020) and ideology (Yazan 2018) have also been highlighted. Varghese (2017) offered the notion of "identity in discourse" to capture the power and ideological struggles in research on L2 teacher identity. The abandonment of NS/NNS classification is the first step to resolve these struggles.

Commitment to Action Taking

One major proposal for overcoming the challenges posed by globalisation of this book is taking action to fulfil the duties to others (as given in Chapter 1 and reiterated throughout Chapters 2 to 4), a major theme of Hegel's (1953, 1977) moral philosophy. The effectiveness of action taking has been empirically confirmed, that participation in intercultural communicative competence (ICC) activities resulted in enhanced moral reasoning (Bowman 2010), development of civic responsibility (Tarsoly and Ćalić 2023; Tsang et al. 2021), and internalisation of cultural values (Taguchi and Roever 2017). Tsang et al. (2023) found that participation in ICC activities enhances both attitudes (e.g., attitudes towards other languages and cultures) and skills (e.g., communicative strategies) of learners. Cross (2020) based his arguments on activity theory and emphasised the actional aspect of identity. According to him, "Identity, 'in activity', brings both dimensions together: A personal (discursive, meaning making) construction of one's self grounded in, and emergent from, the (practical) activity within which that individual is situated as subject" (39). Despite not focusing specifically on morality, the emphasis of action taking in the realisation of one's identity shares similarities with the idea of acting out moral duties, a major theme of this book. In fact, taking responsibility for one's actions, commitment to social justice, as well as critical and active engagement with the community and interdependent world are the key aspects of Oxfam's (2015) definition of GCE. Again, to nurture future L2 teachers on this dimension, teacher educators should be well-versed in this area and embrace the relevant values. Barkhuizen (2019) regards the moral stance and ethical dimension as aspects of L2 teacher identity that cannot be ignored.

RECOMMENDATIONS FOR L2 TEACHER EDUCATION

The post-modern identity is characterised by fluidity and malleability (Donato 2017). In their systematic review of research on L2 teacher identity, Sadeghi and Bahari (2022) found that teachers construct their identity in ways that are person- and context-specific. The implication is that resources and scaffolding should be made available for pre-service and beginning teachers to form an identity that enables them to discharge their responsibilities effectively. Several means for the successful construction of a globalised L2 teacher identity are given in this section.

Reflection

Reflection has been proposed throughout this book for positive L2 identity development in the context of globalisation. Commitment, self-esteem, and self-efficacy are regarded by Richards (2021) as the three aspects of L2 teacher identity. Reflective practices and sensitivity training are ideal ways for examining these three aspects, thus L2 teacher identity. It has also been consistently found that self-reflection contributes to language teacher motivation (Szrogh and Csizér 2020). As life history has been found to contribute to a teacher's linguistic and professional identity (Feng and Kim 2022), personal reflection should be mandatory for L2 teachers to enhance their understanding of their identity, ideology on the role of English (empowerment or marginalisation) (Feng and Kim 2022), and subsequently to improve their teaching in the globalised context.

Regarding the topics for reflection, multilingualism, migration, and the multiplication of identity in relation to globalisation to celebrate cultural diversity (Starkey 2023) are good choices. Critical reflection can be arranged in service learning activities on topics such as openness to other cultures and empathy (Bringle and Clayton 2023). Baker and Fang (2022) recommend reflection to be included in L2 teacher education on intercultural citizenship education. Sun (2021) also reports the effectiveness of using youth literature in engaging pre-service language teachers as reflective thinkers on human rights issues related to globalisation.

Given the increasing understanding of the role of emotion in L2 teacher identity (Harbon 2022; Ng and Cheung 2022; Sadeghi and Bahari 2022), reflection of emotion should be included in the formal L2 teacher training curriculum. Oxfam's (2015) recommendation of critical reflection as a GCE element is equally applicable to L2 teacher education on this aspect.

Awareness Raising and Sensitivity Training on Teacher Emotion

Matsumoto (2018) stresses the importance of training for L2 teachers to be English as a lingua franca (ELF) aware and to gain insights on how to apply ELF concepts and research in their local teaching context. Empirical evidence of a high level of awareness of ELF, including its properties, its influences of globalisation on teaching, and the need to transform teaching approaches among L2 teachers have been identified among teachers (Dewey 2012).

The participants in Mairi et al.'s (2023) study expressed the need for teachers (including English language teachers) to be aware of students' multiple identities in the contemporary globalised education context (Donato 2017). The awareness of multiple identities is also included in the national curriculum of Japan and Vietnam (Nguyen 2022). The concepts of globalisation, cosmopolitanism, and global citizenship originated in Western cultures can be culturally biased towards the Western concept of Enlightenment and are Eurocentric in nature (Starkey 2023). Teachers have the responsibility to inform learners and make them aware of these possible challenges. At the same time, they should impart learners the skills and attitudes to overcome these challenges.

Emotion is a significant part of teacher identity, and it is influenced by micro in-class, meso-institutional, and macro-sociological ecologies of teaching (Nazari et al. 2023). The importance of emotion being identified as a significant element of the identity of English teachers by Nazari et al. (2023) has confirmed the earlier finding of Moser and Kletzenbauer (2019). Emotion in teacher identity has also recently been given more attention by researchers (e.g., Barkhuizen 2019; Jackson and Shirakawa 2020; Sadeghi and Bahari 2022; Shea et al. 2022; Song 2020; Yazan and Lindahl 2020b).

There is a need for the cultivation of cosmopolitan sensibility (Hansen, 2008) which involves emotions and the respect for and recognition of other cultures among learners. Enhancing teachers' self-awareness of interculturality (Perren and Wurr 2015) is equally important. As stated by Feng and Kim (2022), the adoption of English as a global language means that learners need to be more conscious of the form and function in their learning. This is especially true for the existing low level of awareness of variability and multilingualism identified among L2 teachers (Baker and Fang 2022). Tajeddin and Ghaffaryan (2020) in their teacher interviews identified evidence of Iranian English teachers' awareness (despite a low level one) of globalisation through media as part of their teacher identity.

Sensitivity goes hand-in-hand with reflection. This suggests that sensitivity is an outcome of reflection, and at the same time contributes to reflection, and both elements are required for an effective L2 teacher identity.

Service Learning

Service learning has always been a popular means for promoting GCE, and it resonates well with the L2 identity element of a commitment to action taking (Hegel 1953, 1977). The proposal of "border crossing" in the applied linguistic field (e.g., Vinogradov 2015) shares commonness with service learning. Kramsch (2023), for example, introduced five types of "border crossing" for educating global citizens via L2 learning: Experiential borders, disciplinary boundaries, academic borders, national borders, and the third space. While the national border is directly related to overseas exchange programmes, experiential border crossing refers to language educators being multilingual in terms of geographical, linguistic, and cultural borders. Disciplinary border crossing prescribes language educators to adopt a multi-disciplinary perspective, and academic border crossing refers to linking research with practices. Finally, the third space refers to eschewing reductive dichotomies, especially with the emergence of global culture resulting from advancements in digital technologies.

Rauschert (2023) offers an intercultural service learning model that focuses on intercultural encounters within countries and abroad. Particular emphasis is placed on reflection and self-induced action, two recommendations made by many researchers (e.g., Yemini et al. 2019; Bringle and Clayton 2023). Guidelines on the design of out-of-class activities (e.g., Benson 2011) and past successful projects and best practices on service learning on both tertiary students and student teachers are available (e.g., see Bringle and Clayton 2023; see also Perren and Wurr 2015). Rauschert's (2023) comprehensive intercultural service learning model, which emphasises intercultural encounters and reflection, is highly applicable for L2 teacher training for globalisation.

In addition to the above attempts, past projects on the use of digital technology for understanding and constructing L2 teacher identity (e.g.,

Ding and Pawan 2020; Liontas 2020) are not difficult to find, and successful implementations of virtual exchanges for the promotion of critical digital literacies and intercultural communication for Applied Languages degree students (e.g., Giralt et al. 2023; see also Wu et al. in press) have been documented.

Formal Training

Barkhuizen (2019) conducted a research study on the identity of L2 teacher educators and described the results of the qualitative data gathered from interviews. He based his analyses on the framework of Hacker (2008) for researching L2 teacher identity, and the results endorse the validity of the following dimensions of the framework: Teachers and teaching, professional position, and currency (or being informed with the latest trends and knowledge on teaching). Barkhuizen's (2019) findings show the importance of formal training in the formation of L2 teacher educator identity, which has also been highlighted by researchers such as Yazan and Lindahl (2020a). Pre-service teachers' shift from monolithic to plurilithic orientation after undergoing a global English-oriented course has also been reported (Aslan and Altınkaya 2024).

In the study abroad cultural/linguistic immersion programme project implemented by Badenhorst et al. (2023) on raising pre-service teachers' critical consciousness on interculturality described earlier, empirical results show that the programme evoked the fluid identity of one Latina teacher student. The programme also increased participants' understanding of the roles their identities play in the lives of their students. Another finding which is highly related to this chapter is that emotion, relationship building, and empathy were identified as constituting "a foundational tool set for culturally and linguistically responsive ESL practitioners" (9).

Intercultural activities are necessary for nuturing L2 teacher identity and these activities should aim at developing and enhancing the ICC of L2 teachers. Based on the theory of social constructivism, intercultural activities are best conducted through teamwork, with student teachers voicing out their values, negotiating with one another both formally and informally, and finally reaching a consensus on the specific contents required for teacher education. Cross (2022) recommends teamwork emphasising creativity through collaborative efforts of teachers. Baker and Fang (2022) recommend intercultural group work involving students from different parts of the globe to develop intercultural citizenship among learners.

As mentioned earlier, Sun (2021) identified the effectiveness of using English youth literature in pre-service English teacher training for raising student teachers' awareness of the issues of power, privilege, and social justice in the globalised context. Youth literature was also found to be able to activate pre-service teachers to think empathetically on issues such as global and social injustice (Sun 2021). An added positive outcome of their training programme is that pre-service English teachers who participated in the programme expressed they became more confident in implementing similar activities in the language classroom in the future. Harbon (2022) calls for arts-informed elements to cultivate L2 teacher identity, which according to him is able to cater to the emotional needs of intercultural L2 teaching.

The inclusion of GCE in the formal teacher training curriculum is another alternative. Baker and Fang (2022) argue that the lack of formal education on GCE is a major cause for uneven development in intercultural citizenship across the globe. Despite targeting mainly at tertiary students, this argument is equally applicable for L2 student teachers. Integration of service learning in L2 teacher training programmes has been implemented for more than two decades (Minor 2002). Service learning nuanced with intercultural communication brings the benefits of intercultural awareness raising and intercultural citizenship development.

Globalisation has resulted in the design and implementation of L2 curriculum being a complex task which as ever been. Despite its importance, this topic has been neglected in L2 research (Nguyen 2022; see also Wu et al. in press). Unless teacher educators are well aware of and knowledgeable on how globalisaton places demands on L2 learners, an effective curriculum cannot be designed and implemented in the formal, informal, and hidden curriculum. Teacher educators should also be informed of the latest research trends, and how L2 teacher identity changes over time across their career span especially in the context of globalisation.

Recommendations for L2 Teacher Education Research and Theoretical Development

In their systematic review to fill the research gap of a lack of reviews on L2 teacher identity research, Sadeghi and Bahari (2022) concluded that research on L2 teacher identity has largely been focusing generally on how teacher perceptions influence their identity conceptualisation. More research on specific aspects such as how intercultural competence, global citizenship, and morality as introduced in this chapter should be conducted to increase understanding on various aspects of L2 teacher identity, especially for L2 teacher educators.

Research on L2 identity has been characterised by the use of methods based on both the positivist and interpretative paradigms. In addition to the conventional questionnaire surveys, classroom observations, statistical analysis, and model testing which belong to the positivist paradigm, research on L2 identity has adopted methods belonging to the interpretive paradigm such as interviews, content analysis of learner writing and discourses. One recommendation for future research of this book is to systematically review the methodology of research on L2 identity, with the aim of identifying possible advancements. Some groundwork has been undertaken by Norton and McKinney (2011), and more attention should be given to this area. More than two decades ago, Pavlenko and Lantolf (2000) called for a paradigm shift in research on L2 identity and recommended the use of first-person narrative as a research instrument in research on L2 identity (e.g., Norton and McKinney 2011).

The essentialist school focuses on notions such as self-concept (e.g., Benson 2013; Karimova and Csapó 2021), motivation (e.g., Schiller and Dorner 2021), locus of control (Yang et al. 2021), and autonomy (e.g., Little 2020). These notions focusing on individual learners are still attracting substantial amount of attention from researchers to date. Matsumoto (2018) remarks that compared to post-modern theorisation of learner identity, under-theorisation exists in teachers' cultural, intercultural, national, and transnational identities.

L2 identity has close and overlapping relationships with many concepts in educational psychology, to name a few, self, self-concept, self-evaluation, self-regulation, metacognition, autonomy, awareness, consciousness, cognition, and learning strategies. Ivanić (1998) and Joseph (2004) call for clarification in the distinctions and relationships between terms such as "self", "person", "role", "identity", "ethos", "persona", "subject", "subjectivity", and "voice". A better and succinct understanding of L2 identity benefits research and practice on this area. There is a need for future research to demarcate the boundaries between L2 identities with these notions that may be confounding to L2 identity thus posing difficulties. In addition to culture, L2 teacher identity, like L2 identity, is intimately shaped by age, gender, language use, educational background, as well as socio-cultural contexts in which individuals are located. More research on this area can generate findings to increase knowledge in this area.

Conclusion

This chapter began by focusing on the need for L2 teachers to transform their professional identity in facing globalisation. The following essential qualities that constitute L2 teacher identity in the context of globalisation were offered: Awareness and sensitivity of, knowledge of, and respect for diversity of Englishes; good knowledge and command for moral education; a strong sense of empathy to others especially those who are different from oneself; a belief system which is free from a dichotomous NS/NNS classification; and finally, a commitment to action taking. L2 teachers engaging in reflection, intercultural activities, local and overseas on-site or virtual service learning projects, and finally formal training are recommended for fostering these proposed qualities.

Chen et al. (2023) introduced two challenges in their advocacy of Global-Englishes-aware teacher education, which are equally applicable for the nurturing of L2 teacher identity for globalisation. The first challenge is the deeply rooted native-speakerism. Another challenge is the lack of teaching materials. With more attention given to L2 teacher identity, it is hoped that there would be more fruitful discussions to explore how to overcome these challenges.

References

Aboud, Farida. 2020. The effect of E: Learning on EFL teacher identity. *International Journal of English Research* 6 (2): 22–27.
Akkari, Abdeljalil, and Katherine Maleq, eds. 2020. *Global citizenship education: Critical and international perspectives*. Cham: Springer. https://doi.org/10.1007/978-3-030-44617-8.

Aslan, Reyhan and Altınkaya, Zekiye Özer. 2024. Prospective English language teachers' understandings of global English language teaching. *European Journal of Education*: e12631. https://doi.org/10.1111/ejed.12631

Badenhorst, Pauli, Daniela Martin, and Elizabeth Smolcic. 2023. Critical consciousness development for teachers of multilingual learners: A cultural/linguistic immersion program shaping early teaching careers. *Teaching and Teacher Education* 136: 104376. https://doi.org/10.1016/j.tate.2023.104376.

Baker, Will, and Fan Fang. 2022. Intercultural citizenship and the internationalisation of higher education: The role of English language teaching. *Journal of English as a Lingua Franca* 11 (1): 63–75. https://doi.org/10.1515/jelf-2022-2067.

Barkhuizen, Gary. 2017. Language teacher identity research. In Gary Barkhuizen (ed.) *Reflections on language teacher identity research*, 1–11. New York and London: Routledge. https://doi.org/10.4324/9781315643465

Barkhuizen, Gary. 2019. Teacher identity. In Steve Walsh and Steve Mann (eds.) *The Routledge handbook of English language teacher education*, 536–552. Oxon: Routledge. https://doi.org/10.4324/9781315659824

Benson, Phil. 2011. Language learning and teaching beyond the classroom: An introduction to the field. In Phil Benson and Hayo Reinders (eds.) *Beyond the language classroom*, 7–16. UK: Palgrave Macmillan. https://doi.org/10.1057/9780230306790_2

Benson, Phil. 2013. Linguistic self-concept. In Phil Benson, Gary Barkhuizen, Peter Bodycott, and Jill Brown (eds.) *Second language identity in narratives of study abroad*, 72–89. London: Palgrave Macmillan. https://doi.org/10.1057/9781137029423_ 5

Biberman-Shalev, Liat. 2021. Motivational factors for learning and teaching global education. *Teaching and Teacher Education* 106: 103460. https://doi.org/10.1016/j.tate.2021.103460.

Bowman, Nicholas A. 2010. Assessing learning and development among diverse college students. *New Directions for Institutional Research* 145: 53–71. https://doi.org/10.1002/ir.322.

Bringle, Robert G. and Clayton, Patti H. 2023. Challenges to global citizenship education: Nationalism and cosmopolitanism. In Christiane Lütge, Thorsten Merse, and Petra Rauschert (eds.) *Global citizenship in foreign language education: Concepts, practices, connections*, 79–106. New York and London: Routledge. https://doi.org/10.4324/9781003183839-6

Cavanagh, Claire. 2020. The role of English in global citizenship. *Journal of Global Citizenship & Equity Education* 7 (1): 1–23. https://doi.org/10.13140/RG.2.2.21671.60328

Chen, Ziyin, Xiaojuan Chen, and Fan Fang. 2023. Global Englishes and teacher education: Present cases and future directions. *RELC Journal* 54 (3): 873–880. https://doi.org/10.1177/00336882211044872.

Choi, Lee Jin. 2018. Embracing identities in second language learning: Current status and future directions. *Problems of Education in the 21st Century* 76 (6): 800–815. https://doi.org/10.33225/pec/18.76.800

Coldron, John, and Robin Smith. 1999. Active location in teachers' construction of their professional identities. *Journal of Curriculum Studies* 31 (6): 711–726. https://doi.org/10.1080/002202799182954.

Cooper, Ayanna C. and Bryan, Kisha C. 2020. Reading, writing, and race: Sharing the narratives of black TESOL professionals. In Bedrettin Yazan and Kristen Lindahl (eds.) *Language teacher identity in TESOL teacher education and practice as identity work*, 125–142. New York and Oxon: Routledge. https://doi.org/10.4324/9780429342875

Cross, Russell. 2020. The 'subject' of Freeman & Johnson's reconceived knowledge base of second language teacher education. *Language Teaching Research* 24 (1): 37–48. https://doi.org/10.1177/1362168818777521.

Davidson, Rachel, and Yongcan Liu. 2020. Reaching the world outside: Cultural representation and perceptions of global citizenship in Japanese elementary school English textbooks. *Language, Culture and Curriculum* 33 (1): 32–49. https://doi.org/10.1080/07908318.2018.1560460.

De Ruyter, Doret J. and Spiecker, Ben. 2008. The world citizen travels with a different view. In Michael Peters, Alan Britton, and Harry Blee (eds.) *Global citizenship education: Philosophy, theory and pedagogy*, 351–363. Rotterdam: Sense. https://doi.org/10.1163/9789087903756_023

Demuth, Constanze. 2018. Liberalism's all-inclusive promise of freedom and its illiberal effects: A critique of the concept of globalization. In Conch Roldán, Daniel Brauer, and Johannes Rohbeck (eds.) *Philosophy of globalization*, 63–77. Berlin and Boston: Walter de Gruyter. https://doi.org/10.1515/978311 0492415-006

Denfeld, Annette-Pascale., Esther T. Canrinus, and Inger Marie Dalehefte. 2023. Teacher identity in work with students' psychosocial environment: A systematic review of quantitative research. *Psychology in the Schools* 60 (12): 5041–5061. https://doi.org/10.1002/pits.23001.

Dewey, Martin. 2012. Towards a post-normative approach: Learning the pedagogy of ELF. *Journal of English as a Lingua Franca* 1 (1): 141–170. https://doi.org/10.1515/jelf-2012-0007.

Ding, Ai-Chu Elisha and Pawan, Faridah. 2020. Multimodal identity construction of technology-using language teachers via stance taking in an online learning space. In Bedrettin Yazan and Kristen Lindahl (eds.) *Language teacher identity in TESOL teacher education and practice as identity work*, 83–100. New York and Oxon: Routledge. https://doi.org/10.4324/978042934 2875

Donato, Richard. 2017. Becoming a language teaching professional: What's identity got to do with it? In Gary Barkhuizen (eds.) *Reflections on language teacher identity research*, 24–30. New York and London: Routledge. https://doi.org/10.4324/9781315643465

Fang, Fan (Gabriel). 2020. Glocalization, English as a lingua franca and ELT: Reconceptualizing identity and models for ELT in China. In Bedrettin Yazan and Kristen Lindahl (eds.) *Criticality, teacher identity, and (in)equity in English language teaching*, 23–39. https://doi.org/10.1007/978-3-319-729 20-6_2

Feng, Maomao, and Hoe Kyeung Kim. 2022. EFL teachers' spatial construction of linguistic identities for sustainable development in globalization. *Sustainability* 14: 4532. https://doi.org/10.3390/su14084532.

García, Ofelia. 2016. Critical multilingual language awareness and teacher education. In Jasone Cenoz, Durk Gorter, and Stephen May (eds.) *Language awareness and multilingualism*, 263–280. Cham: Springer. https://doi.org/10.1007/978-3-319-02325-0_30-1

Gayton, Angela Mary. 2016. Perceptions about the dominance of English as a global language: Impact on foreign-language teachers' professional identity. *Journal of Language, Identity & Education* 15 (4): 230–244. https://doi.org/10.1016/10.1080/15348458.2016.1194209.

Giralt, Marta, Murray, Liam, and Benini, Silvia. 2023. Global citizenship and virtual exchange practices promoting critical digital literacies and intercultural competence in language education. In Christiane Lütge, Thorsten Merse, and Petra Rauschert (eds.) *Global citizenship in foreign language education: Concepts, practices, connections*, 151–173. New York and London: Routledge. https://doi.org/10.4324/9781003183839

Hacker, Penelope Ann. 2008. *Understanding the nature of language teacher educator learning: substance, narrative essence and contextual reality.* Unpublished thesis, University of Auckland, New Zealand.

Hansen, David T. 2008. Curriculum and the idea of a cosmopolitan inheritance. *Journal of Curriculum Studies* 40 (3): 289–312. https://doi.org/10.1080/00220270802036643.

Harbon, Lesley. 2022. An arts-informed teacher identity for intercultural language teaching. In Karim Sadeghi and Farah Ghaderi (eds.) *Theory and practice in second language teacher identity*, 89–102. Cham: Springer. https://doi.org/10.1007/978-3-031-13161-5_3

Hegel, Georg Wilhelm Friedrich. 1953. *The philosophy of right*. Translated by Thomas Malcolm Knox. Oxford: Oxford University Press.

Hegel, Georg Wilhelm Friedrich. 1977. *Phenomenology of spirit*. Translated by Arnold Vincent Miller. Oxford: Oxford University Press.

Houghton, Stephanie Ann. 2020. Overcoming native-speakerism through post-native-speakerist pedagogy: Gaps between teacher and pre-service English teacher priorities. In Stephanie Ann Houghton and Jérémie Bouchard (eds.) *Native-speakerism: Its resilience and undoing*, 89–113. Singapore: Springer. https://doi.org/10.1007/978-981-15-5671-5_5

Ivanič, Roz. 1998. *Writing and identity: The discoursal construction of identity in academic writing*. Amsterdam and Philadelphia: John Benjamins. https://doi.org/10.1075/swll.5

Jackson, Daniel O. and Shirakawa, Tomoya. 2020. Identity, noticing, and emotion among preservice English language teachers. In Bedrettin Yazan and Kristen Lindahl (eds.) *Language teacher identity in TESOL teacher education and practice as identity work*, 197–212. New York and Oxon: Routledge. https://doi.org/10.4324/9780429342875

Joseph, John E. 2004. *Language and identity*. London: Palgrave Macmillan. https://doi.org/10.1057/9780230503427.

Kant, Immanuel. 1957. *Perpetual peace*. Englewood Cliffs: Macmillan.

Kant, Immanuel. 1970. Metaphysics of morals. In *Kant's political writings*. Translated by Hugh Barr Nisbet and edited by Hans Reiss, 131–175. Cambridge: Cambridge University Press.

Karimova, Könü., and Benő Csapó. 2021. The relationship between cognitive and affective dimensions of reading self-concept with reading achievement in English and Russian. *Journal of Advanced Academics* 32 (3): 324–353. https://doi.org/10.1177/1932202X219959.

Karpava, Sviatlana. (ed.) 2023. *Handbook of research on language teacher identity*. Hershey: IGI Global. https://doi.org/10.4018/978-1-6684-7275-0

Kaya, Yunus, Sevda Arslan, Atiy Erbaş, Berile Nisa Yaşar, and Gülhan Erkuş. Küçükkelepçe. 2021. The effect of ethnocentrism and moral sensitivity on intercultural sensitivity in nursing students, descriptive cross-sectional research study. *Nurse Education Today* 100: 104867. https://doi.org/10.1016/j.nedt.2021.104867.

King, Jim and Ng, Kwan-Yee Sarah. 2018. Teacher emotions and the emotional labour of second language teaching. In Sarah Mercer and Achilleas Kostoulas (eds.) *Language teacher psychology*, 140–157. Bristol, Blue Ridge Summit: Multilingual Matters. https://doi.org/10.21832/9781783099467

Kramsch, Claire. 2023. Re-imagining foreign language education in a post-COVID-19 world. In Christiane Lütge, Thorsten Merse, and Petra Rauschert (eds.) *Global citizenship in foreign language education: Concepts, practices, connections*, 15–40. New York and London: Routledge. https://doi.org/10.4324/9781003183839-3

Kutoba, Ryuko. 2018. Unpacking research and practice in world Englishes and second language acquisition. *World Englishes* 37: 93–105. https://doi.org/10.1111/weng.12305.

Lee, Eunjeong, and A. Suresh. Canagarajah. 2019a. The connection between transcultural dispositions and translingual practices. *Journal of Multicultural Discourses* 14: 14–28. https://doi.org/10.1080/17447143.2018.1501375.

Lee, Eunjeong, and A. Suresh. Canagarajah. 2019b. Beyond native and nonnative: Translingual dispositions for more inclusive teacher identity in language and literacy education. *Journal of Language, Identity & Education* 18 (6): 352–363. https://doi.org/10.1080/15348458.2019.1674148.

Lee, Jerry Won and Jenks, Christopher. 2016. Doing translingual dispositions: Considerations from a US-Hong Kong partnership. *College Composition and Communication* 68: 317–344. https://doi.org/10.58680/ccc201628883

Leung, Alex Ho-Cheong and Yip, Timothy. 2020. Reality check: Identity struggle and experiences of NESTs living and teaching abroad. In Bedrettin Yazan and Kristen Lindahl (eds.) *Language teacher identity in TESOL teacher education and practice as identity work*, 161–178. New York and Oxon: Routledge. https://doi.org/10.4324/9780429342875-13

Li, Cuicui. 2022. Perpetuating student inequality? The discrepancy and disparity of global citizenship education in Chinese rural & urban schools. *Asia Pacific Education Review* 23: 389–401. https://doi.org/10.1007/s12564-021-09708-7.

Liontas, John I. 2020. Understanding language teacher identity: Digital discursive spaces in English teacher education and development. In Bedrettin Yazan and Kristen Lindahl (eds.) *Language teacher identity in TESOL teacher education and practice as identity work*, 65–82. New York and Oxon: Routledge. https://doi.org/10.4324/9780429342875

Little, David. 2020. Language learner autonomy: Rethinking language teaching. *Language Teaching* 2020: 1–10. https://doi.org/10.1017/S026144482000048 8.

Mairi, Salam, Johanna Gruber, Sarah Mercer, Alina Schartner, Jan Ybema, Tony Young, and Cor van der Meer. 2023. Teacher educators' perspectives on global citizenship education and multilingual competences. *Journal of Multilingual and Multicultural Development*. https://doi.org/10.1080/01434632.2023.2170388.

Matsumoto, Yumi. 2018. Teachers' identities as 'non-native' speakers: do they matter in English as a lingua franca interactions? In Bedrettin Yazan and Kristen Lindahl (eds.) *Criticality, teacher identity, and (in)equity in English language teaching*, 57–80. https://doi.org/10.1007/978-3-319-72920-6_9

Minor, James. 2002. Incorporating service learning into ESOL programs. *TESOL Journal* 11 (4): 10–14. https://doi.org/10.1002/j.1949-3533.2002.tb00103.x.

Mirzaei, Azizullah and Parhizkar, Reza. 2021. The interplay of l2 pragmatics and learner identity as a social, complex process: A poststructuralist perspective. *TESL-EJ* 25 (1). https://tesl-ej.org/pdf/ej97/a3.pdf

Moser, Alia and Kletzenbauer, Petra. 2019. Thinking outside the box: The impact of globalization on English language teachers in Austria. In Achilleas Kostoulas (ed.) *Challenging boundaries in language education, second language learning and teaching*, 165–181. Switzerland AG: Springer Nature. https://doi.org/10.1007/978-3-030-17057-8_10

Nazari, Mostafa, Mohammad Nabi Karimi, and Peter I. De Costa. 2023. Emotion and identity construction in teachers of young learners of English: An ecological perspective. *System* 112: 102972. https://doi.org/10.1016/j.system.2022.102972.

Ng, Chiew Hong and Cheung, Yin Ling. 2022. Second language teacher identity: A synthesis of reflections from applied linguists. In Karim Sadeghi and Farah Ghaderi (eds.) *Theory and practice in second language teacher identity*, 59–74. Cham: Springer. https://doi.org/10.1007/978-3-031-13161-5_5

Nguyen, Bich-Phuong Thi. 2022. English language teacher education through the kaleidoscope of global citizenship: Japan and Vietnam in comparative perspective. In Clementine M. Msengi, Grace K. Lartey, and Katherine R. Sprott (eds.) *Contemporary issues in multicultural and global education*, 143–166. Hershey: IGI Global. https://doi.org/10.4018/978-1-7998-7404-1.ch009

Norton, Bonny. (2021) Identity in language learning and teaching. In Hassan Mohebbi and Christine Coombe (eds.) *Research questions in language education and applied linguistics*, 81–85. Cham: Springer. https://doi.org/10.1007/978-3-030-79143-8_15

Norton, Bonny and McKinney, Carolyn. 2011. An identity approach to second language acquisition. In Dwight Atkinson (ed.) *Alternative approaches to second language acquisition*, 73–94. Abingdon: Routledge. https://doi.org/10.4324/9780203830932

Oxfam. 2015. *Education for global citizenship*. Oxford: Oxfam.

Oxley, Laura, and Paul Morris. 2013. Global citizenship: A typology for distinguishing its multiple conceptions. *British Journal of Educational Studies* 61: 301–325. https://doi.org/10.1080/00071005.2013.798393.

Pavlenko, Aneta, and James Lantolf. 2000. Second language learning as participation and the (re) construction of selves. In *Sociocultural theory and second language learning*, ed. James P. Lantolf, 155–177. Oxford: Oxford University Press.

Perren, James M. and Wurr, Adrian J. (eds.) (2015) *Learning the language of global citizenship: Strengthening service-learning in TESOL*. Champaign: Common Ground Publishing. https://doi.org/10.18848/978-1-61229-815-3/CGP

Rauschert, Petra. 2023. Intercultural service learning reframed: A comprehensive model and its practical implementation in the foreign language classroom. In Christiane Lütge, Thorsten Merse, and Petra Rauschert (eds.) *Global citizenship in foreign language education: Concepts, practices, connections*, 109–127. New York and London: Routledge. https://doi.org/10.4324/978100318 3839-8

Richards, Jack C. 2021. Teacher, learner and student–teacher identity in TESOL. *RELC Journal*. https://doi.org/10.1177/0033688221991308.

Sadeghi, Karim and Bahari, Akbar. 2022. Second language teacher identity: A systematic review. In Karim Sadeghi and Farah Ghaderi (eds.) *Theory and practice in second language teacher identity*, 11–30. Cham: Springer. https://doi.org/10.1007/978-3-031-13161-5_2

Schattle, Hans. 2008. Education for global citizenship: Illustrations of ideological pluralism and adaptation. *Journal of Political Ideologies* 13: 73–94. https://doi.org/10.1080/13569310701822263.

Schattle, Hans. 2009. Global citizenship in theory and practice. In Ross Lewin (ed.) *The handbook of practice and research in study abroad: Higher education and the quest for global citizenship*, 3–20. New York: Routledge. https://doi.org/10.4324/9780203876640

Schiller, Emese and Helga, Dorner. 2021. Factors influencing senior learners' language learning motivation. A Hungarian perspective. *Journal of Adult Learning, Knowledge and Innovation* 5 (1): 12–21. https://doi.org/10.1556/2059.2020.00003

Schissel, Jamie L. and Stephens, Crissa. 2020. Anti-oppressive pedagogy in language teacher education: A collaborative case study of identity texts. In Bedrettin Yazan and Kristen Lindahl (eds.) *Language teacher identity in TESOL teacher education and practice as identity work*, 143–160. New York and Oxon: Routledge. https://doi.org/10.4324/9780429342875-12

Shani, Giorgio. 2003. 'The liberal project': Globalization, modernity and identity. *Ritsumeikan Annual Review of International Studies* 2: 37–57.

Shea, Kate, Li, Shi, and Kayi-Aydar, Hayriye. 2022. Understanding positional identities of ESL teachers in response to identity conflicts through an analysis of emotions and agency. In Karim Sadeghi and Farah Ghaderi (eds.) *Theory and practice in second language teacher identity*, 277–292. Cham: Springer. https://doi.org/10.1007/978-3-031-13161-5_19

Song, Juyoung. 2020. Teacher emotion as pedagogy: The role of emotions in negotiating pedagogy and teacher identity. In Bedrettin Yazan and Kristen Lindahl (eds.) *Language teacher identity in TESOL teacher education and practice as identity work*, 181–196. New York and Oxon: Routledge. https://doi.org/10.4324/9780429342875

Starkey, Hugh. 2023. Challenges to global citizenship education: Nationalism and cosmopolitanism. In Christiane Lütge, Thorsten Merse, and Petra

Rauschert (eds.) *Global citizenship in foreign language education: Concepts, practices, connections*, 63–78. New York and London: Routledge. https://doi.org/10.4324/9781003183839-5

Sun, Lina. 2021. Transforming pre-service EFL teacher education through critical cosmopolitan literacies: Voices from Mainland China. *Teaching in Higher Education*. https://doi.org/10.1080/13562517.2021.2015753.

Sun, Xiaoan. 2020. Towards a common framework for global citizenship education: A critical review of UNESCO's conceptual framework of global citizenship education. In Xudong Zhu, Jiayong Li, Mang Li, Qiang Liu, and Hugh Starkey (eds.) *Education and mobilities, perspectives on rethinking and reforming education*, 263–277. Singapore: Springer Nature. https://doi.org/10.1007/978-981-13-9031-9_15

Sun, Tingting, and Adcharawan Buripakdi. 2023. Unpacking Chinese primary school English teachers' perceptions: Personal blockers and enablers in global citizenship education. *Asia Pacific Journal of Education*. https://doi.org/10.1080/02188791.2023.2235918.

Szrogh, Bence, and Kata Csizér. 2020. The role of attitudes, selves and experiences in shaping foreign language teachers' motivation: The comparative results of three questionnaire studies. In *DEAL 2020: A snapshot of diversity in English applied linguistics*, ed. Csaba Kálmán, 233–251. Budapest: Eötvös Loránd University.

Taguchi, Naoko, and Carsten Roever. 2017. *Second language pragmatics*. Oxford: Oxford University Press.

Tajeddin, Zia, and Susan Ghaffaryan. 2020. Language teachers' intercultural identity in the critical context of cultural globalization and its metaphoric realization. *Journal of Intercultural Communication Research* 49 (3): 263–281. https://doi.org/10.1080/17475759.2020.1754884.

Tarsoly, Eszter and Ćalić, Jelena. 2023. Language learning and community engagement for global citizenship. In Christiane Lütge, Thorsten Merse, and Petra Rauschert (eds.) *Global citizenship in foreign language education: Concepts, practices, connections*, 267–287. New York and London: Routledge. https://doi.org/10.4324/9781003183839-16

Tsang, Art, Scott Aubrey, and Rui Yuan. 2023. Multiculturalism and multilingualism in higher education: Intercultural activity participation and opportunities for language learning. *International Journal of Multilingualism*. https://doi.org/10.1080/14790718.2022.2164769.

Tsang, Art, Min Yang, and Rui Yuan. 2021. The relationships between participation in intercultural activities on campus, whole-person development, and academic achievement: A mixed-methods study. *Journal of Multilingual and Multicultural Development*. https://doi.org/10.1080/01434632.2021.1963121.

UNESCO. 2015. *Global citizenship education: Topics and learning objectives.* Paris: UNESCO.

UNESCO. 2016. *The ABCs of global citizenship education.* Retrieved 14 April 2024, from https://unesdoc.unesco.org/ark:/48223/pf0000248232

UNESCO. 2021. *Global citizenship education.* Retrieved 14 April 2024, from https://en.unesco.org/themes/gced

Varghese, Manka M. 2017. Language teacher educator identity and language teacher identity: Towards a social justice perspective. In Gary Barkhuizen (eds.) *Reflections on language teacher identity research,* 16–26. New York and London: Routledge. https://doi.org/10.4324/9781315643465

Veugelers, Wiel. 2011. The moral and the political in global citizenship: Appreciating differences in education. *Globalisation, Societies and Education* 9: 473–485. https://doi.org/10.1080/14767724.2011.605329.

Vinogradov, Patsy. 2015. Border crossings: Researching across contexts for teacher professional development. In Simon Borg and Hugo Santiago Sanchez (eds.) *International perspectives on teacher research,* 70–86. London: Palgrave Macmillan. https://doi.org/10.1057/9781137376220_6

Wang, Ying. 2020. *Language ideologies in the Chinese context: Orientations to English as a lingua franca.* Boston: Walter de Gruyter. https://doi.org/10.1515/9781501503702.

Widodo, Handoyo Puji, Fan Fang, and Tariq Elyas. 2020. The construction of language teacher professional identity in the Global Englishes territory: 'we are legitimate language teachers.' *Asian Englishes* 22 (3): 309–316. https://doi.org/10.1080/13488678.2020.1732683.

Wu, Manfred Man-fat. 2020. Second language teaching for global citizenship. *Globalisation, Societies and Education* 18 (3): 330–342. https://doi.org/10.1080/14767724.2019.1693349.

Wu, Manfred Man-fat, Römhild, Ricardo, and Nishizaki, Mona. In press. Teaching English as an international language for global citizenship. In Nicola Galloway and Ali Fuad Selvi (eds.) *The Routledge handbook of English as an international language.* Routledge.

Yang, Hong Mian, Yun Li, Meng Xuan Zhang, Vivienne Y. K. Tao, Kwok Kit Tong, and Anise M. S. Wu. 2021. Locus of control, coping flexibility, and post-migration growth among mainland Chinese university students in Macao. *International Journal of Intercultural Relations* 85: 13–25. https://doi.org/10.1016/j.ijintrel.2021.08.012.

Yazan, Bedrettin. 2018. A conceptual framework to understand language teacher identities. *Journal of Second Language Teacher Identities* 1 (1): 22–48. https://doi.org/10.1558/slte.24908.

Yazan, Bedrettin, and Kristen Lindahl, eds. 2020a. *Language teacher identity in TESOL: Teacher education and practice as identity work.* New York and London: Routledge. https://doi.org/10.4324/9780429342875.

Yazan, Bedrettin, and Kristen Lindahl. 2020b. Language teacher learning and practice as identity work: An overview of the field and this volume. In *Language teacher identity in TESOL: Teacher education and practice as identity work*, ed. Bedrettin Yazan and Kristen Lindahl, 1–10. New York: Routledge.

Yemini, Miri, Felisa Tibbitts, and Heela Goren. 2019. Trends and caveats: Review of literature on global citizenship education in teacher training. *Teaching and Teacher Education* 77: 77–89. https://doi.org/10.1016/j.tate.2018.09.014.

You, Xiaoye. 2016. *Cosmopolitan English and transliteracy*. Carbondale: Southern Illinois University Press. https://doi.org/10.1111/weng.12353.

PART III

Conclusion

CHAPTER 7

Conclusion

Abstract Globalisation is a significant part of contemporary life, and its influences on second language (L2) identity have been profound and diverse. L2 identity affects learner behaviours related to L2 learning as well as attitudes towards L2 learning and those who speak the target language. This book has undertaken the task of discussing ways in which globalisation influences L2 identity, the opportunities and challenges globalisation has brought to L2 identity, and the dilemmas of L2 identity in facing globalisation. Discussions on how L2 autonomy has been influenced by globalisation and the requirements for transformation of learners and teachers have been included. One major conclusion of this book is that globalisation has called for moral education for L2 identity. Future endeavours, whether on theoretical development, pedagogical advancements, or research on L2 identity, should put due consideration on morality.

Keywords Globalisation · Opportunities · Challenges · L2 autonomy · L2 identity · Moral education

INTRODUCTION

Globalisation has radically transformed many aspects of contemporary life. Akkari and Maleq (2020) succinctly outlined the unprecedented influences of globalisation, stating that it "has not only deeply impacted societies, the world economy, information and communication technologies but also the field of education" (p. 207). Despite the substantial amount of literature on the influences of globalisation on education (e.g., Rizvi et al. 2022), scant attention has been given to how globalisation has affected L2 learning (see Wu 2020). Discussions to date in this area either focus solely on L2 identity only (e.g., Block 2014) or on specific contexts such as study abroad (Benson et al. 2013; Malovrh 2023).

L2 identity is a key construct not only in the acquisition of an L2 but also in many other aspects of individuals' well-being. Individuals' learning experiences contribute to the construction of their L2 identity, and their L2 identity constructed over the years in turn influences their perceptions of L2 learning. The previous chapters have discussed how globalisation influences L2 identity, as well as the opportunities and challenges globalisation has brought for the construction and maintenance of L2 identity. The increasing extent of cultural exchange due to globalisation creates tensions on self, especially in terms of morality. This is because language and value are intimately related, and there are conflicting demands in terms of the morality of different cultures. Therefore, morality, a dimension that has almost been completely neglected, is proposed to be included as a key component in fostering L2 identity at the outset of this book. As autonomy is an integral part of identity and a contributor to successful language learning, how to reconceptualise and foster L2 autonomy in the age of globalisation is discussed in Chapter 4 of this book. Finally, globalisation has generated new demands for L2 teachers (Wu 2024), and teachers need to transform their identity in order to stay effective in their teaching. This book has proposed the essential qualities that constitute effective L2 teacher identity in the context of globalisation.

In sum, this book aims to offer information, discussions, and resources to enhance existing understanding of how globalisation influences positively and negatively the L2 identity of learners and teachers. The information included in this book may also enable higher education management and language policy leaders to understand how globalisation influences the L2 identity of learners, which enables them to formulate policies and curricula that can nurture the positive development of L2 identity of students.

In this final chapter, a summary of arguments included in previous chapters, the conclusion, recommendations, and future directions in terms of theoretical development, pedagogy, and future research related to L2 identity in the globalisation context are introduced.

Summary of Major Arguments

Part One of this book introduces the background and motivation for writing this book by focusing on the impacts of globalisation on L2 identity. The introductory chapter sets the stage for subsequent discussions and offers the background information for writing this book. The meaning of globalisation and the conceptualisation of morality adopted in this book are introduced. These are followed by accounts on how globalisation has resulted in the need for global citizenship and human rights. Finally, the roles of morality in L2 identity are described. The aim is to draw attention to this relatively neglected area and to locate morality in the context of globalisation.

The second part of this book focuses on the core themes of this book as its title suggests, globalisation's positive and negative impacts. Chapters 2–4 discuss the opportunities and challenges for globalised L2 identity; dilemmas of L2 identity in globalisation and the Hegelian solution to morality; and the recommendation of the need for infusing L2 identity with moral elements for globalisation.

In Chapter 2, the following opportunities for globalised L2 identity are described: the English classroom as an ideal niche for global identity construction, fluid and flexible post-structural identity, and material benefits brought by globalisation. The challenges discussed in this chapter are globalisation's neglect of individual subjectivity, the rise of nationalism, homogenisation of culture, and naïve cosmopolitanism. The inclusion of human rights and duties to others in L2 education, provision of expression of voice for learners for cultural alternatives, the inclusion of writer identity in the L2 writing curriculum, grammar teaching for construction of globalised L2 identity, and finally the provision of a more balanced description of English native-speaking cultures and those of other cultures in L2 textbooks are the means proposed for responding to globalisation for positive development and maintenance of L2 identity.

Chapter 3 continues the discussions of Chapter 2 on morality and introduces four dilemmas of self raised by Giddens (2006), which are equally applicable for L2 identity: Unification vs Fragmentation; Powerlessness vs Appropriation; Authority vs Uncertainty; and finally, Personalised vs Commercial experience. Hegel emphasises pure duty, and more importantly, its actualisation in his anthro-political philosophy, and Hegelian morality can empower individuals in resolving the tensions in the four dilemmas. Chapter 4 continues the discussions of Chapter 3, and examines how globalisation influences the L2 identity of learners from a Hegelian perspective. As reiterated throughout the book, globalisation places unprecedented challenges on morality, as the mingling of diverse cultures around the globe causes tensions in morality. Hegelian morality is proposed in this book to achieve the following moral endeavours: Overcoming inequality, overcoming prejudice, promoting social justice, recognition of the diversity of identities, promoting critical literacy, providing education on the importance of national borders for cultural identity preservation, and global mutual recognition.

Chapters 5 and 6 discuss two aspects that are highly related to L2 identity in the globalisation context. They are how globalisation has influenced L2 autonomy and L2 teacher identity. In Chapter 5, the emerging need to reconceptualise L2 autonomy coined in the 1980s caused by the radical and large-scale contextual changes by globalisation and increasing multilingualism over the years has been pointed out. Hegelian philosophy is suggested as an ideal means for the necessary reconceptualisation. As learners, L2 teachers need to transform their identity in order to stay effective in their profession in the globalised context. Chapter 6 highlights the following essential qualities that constitute L2 teacher identity in the context of globalisation: Awareness and sensitivity of, knowledge of, and respect for diversity of Englishes; a good knowledge and command of intercultural communications; a strong sense of empathy to others especially those who are different from oneself; and a belief system free from a dichotomous native-speaker/non-native-speaker classification. L2 teachers engaging in reflection, intercultural activities, local and overseas on-site or virtual service learning projects, and formal training are recommended for the nurturing of these qualities.

Conclusion

Since Kant (1957) introduced his seminal idea of cosmopolitanism which emphasised human rights more than two centuries ago in the Enlightenment era, globalisation has been exerting influences on various parts of the world, individuals' lives, and global ideology. With the rapid technological advancements in recent decades, the repercussions of globalisation have become increasingly acute. As the discussions in this book have shown, globalisation has shaken the conventional moral foundation globally and has generated tensions for self-identity, including L2 identity. However, despite its significance, this aspect has been largely neglected. Therefore, morality, specifically from the Kantian coupled with the Hegelian one, is proposed to be included as a key component in fostering L2 identity. L2 identity is a concoction of value, knowledge, and emotion, and neglecting any one of these dimension in nurturing L2 identity is deemed to lead to negative outcomes.

Despite having been stated in the introductory chapter, the reasons for adopting Kant's conceptualisation of morality need to be re-emphasised in this final chapter. There are three reasons for the adoption of Kant's philosophy on globalisation as the conceptual framework of this book. The first is that he is a pioneer in the philosophical discussions on globalisaton and his theory on globalisation has a solid philosophical foundation. The second reason is that his philosophy on globalisation embraces morality and human rights, which is highly pertinent for overcoming the challenges brought by globalisation. Kant's theories on morality, especially the duties to others, suffer from the limitation of being an empty formalism. Therefore, the emphasis on realisation of pure duty through action taking of Hegel (1953, 1977), a post-Kantian German Idealist philosopher who developed his theory partly to overcome Kant's inadequacy, has been included in the proposal of this book. The inclusion of Hegelian morality in L2 identity, as suggested in Chapter 4, can overcome inequality, prejudice, and social injustice. At the same time, Hegelian morality should form the basis for the construction of multiple identities, re-demarcation of national borders, redefinition of the roles of non-state bodies, and the achievement of global mutual recognition.

Pashby et al. (2020) interpret the term "global citizenship" as paradoxical because the word "global" connotes universality and "citizenship" particularity. Tarozzi and Torres (2016) also describe the tensions in using the two words in combination. The same paradoxical nature can be found in the term "global L2 identity" discussed in this book. Globalisation exerts homogenising influences on the L2 identity of learners in terms of beliefs, values, and attitudes. At the same time, as its name suggests, L2 identity refers to the unique characteristics of one's self in terms of L2 learning. These two notions seem to be antagonistic to each other and create tensions for L2 learners. In fact, L2 identity involves constant struggles (Wu 2024) both for learners and teachers.

Major Recommendations for Developments on Theory, Research, and Pedagogy for L2 Identity

Having discussed globalisation's effects on the L2 identity of students and language teachers as well as the need for pedagogical transformation, the remainder of this chapter offers some suggestions on the theoretical, research, and practical levels based on the discussions made in the previous chapters. Details are given below.

Theory

Both Chapters 1 and 3 have emphasised that human rights from the Kantian perspective and Hegelian duties to others and its realisation through taking actions should be included in nurturing L2 identity. The inclusion of human rights and duties to others in L2 education was reiterated in Chapter 2. On a broader level, more reflections on the roles of L2 teaching from a moral and philosophical perspective such as those by Wu (2023) and those focusing on globalisation (e.g., Wu in press; Wu et al. in press) should be undertaken. Most importantly, stronger advocacy for morality as a means for positive L2 identity development needs to be made in the future.

As described in the previous chapters, the concept of global competence, despite being underdeveloped, is potentially useful to complement the theoretical development of the Hegelian perspective of morality for globalised L2 identity. Mansilla and Wilson (2020) have identified that global competence is highly consistent with Chinese culture, and can be extended to cover the moral virtuous dispositions of Chinese culture. The relevant elements of global competence are dedication to understanding the world, understanding and relating to others harmoniously, communicating and interacting with others mindfully, and finally taking action in collaboration with others harmoniously for a better world. These four virtues share the notions of human rights (which include universal right, cosmopolitan right, and hospitality right); duties to others cosmopolitan sensibility (the respect for and recognition of other cultures), and taking actions to actualise the duties to others proposed in this book. However, Engel et al. (2019) expressed that this concept of global competence is based on neoliberal education policy which is at odds with notions of social justice and universal human rights. In addition, it suffers from underdevelopment in terms of operationalisation and measurement (Kabir et al. 2022; Schenker 2019; Sugiyanto, 2021) as well as empirical support received (Parmigiani et al. 2022). More attention should be given to this area.

A remark offered by Akkari and Maleq (2020) on global citizenship education (GCE) is particularly relevant here. In the conclusion of their book, they (Akkari and Maleq 2020) call for more comparative and critical research on challenging the Western ideological bias underlying the assumption of GCE. This remark equally applies to the theoretical development of L2 identity in the globalised context, especially that research and theoretical development on L2 have been heavily nuanced with the Western ideological paradigm.

Some ideological gaps remain to be filled regarding L2 identity and globalisation. The primordial gap is the antagonistic nature between elitism emphasised by neoliberalism and the core value of equality and social justice of globalisation, global citizenship, and human rights (e.g., Zajda 2020). L2 professionals also need to step out from their conventional academic territories and become more embracing of ideological currents such as the need for morality and philosophy as proposed in this book. A paradigm shift to L2 theories in response to globalisation is necessary. Matsumoto (2018), on the other hand, pointed out the undertheorisation of teachers' cultural, intercultural, national, and transnational identities.

Pedagogy and Teacher Training

One strength of this book is that concrete recommendations in terms of pedagogy both for L2 learners and L2 teachers are offered despite the philosophical nature of the discussions. As described earlier in this chapter, five pedagogical recommendations are made for the positive development of L2 identity in Chapter 2. In Chapter 3, the discoursal approach or L2 learners' awareness raising of how language and culture shape their

L2 identity, a negotiated approach for the construction of a globalised identity, and mutual recognition are given. Chapter 5 reiterates the importance of mutual recognition and a negotiated approach for L2 autonomy and taking into consideration culture in L2 autonomy.

Language planning and policy exert direct influences on pedagogy. There is a need for further investigation into how ideologies, social inequalities, political realignments, and self-identity of individuals are influenced by language planning and policy. Wu (in press) calls for a revamp of L2 teacher education curricula in response to the emerging requirements such as accreditation, benchmarking of course materials, and standardisation of assessment brought by internationalisaton of higher education. These transformations can enhance the recognition of L2 teacher training qualifications at the international level. However, Wu (in press) warns that internationalisation of teacher training curriculum tends to delocalise native culture (Demuth 2018), and may cause teacher resistance and nationalism (Mallinson 2021). A balance on meeting international standards, preserving local culture and taking into consideration local needs is highly desirable. The inadequacies of conventional assessments under the influence of globalisation and the need for incorporating intercultural communicative competence into assessment are also issues to address (Wu 2024).

Intimately related to language policy are the roles of stakeholders including learners, teachers, school management, government, community, commercial bodies such as publishers, and supranational organisations such as UNESCO and Oxfam in the promotion of global citizenship, globalisation, human rights, and sustainability.

In Chapter 5, it was recommended that teacher training is the starting point for moral and political aspects of L2 autonomy. Teacher reflection was suggested to be a core means for nurturing L2 teacher identity for globalisation. Four qualities were raised in Chapter 6 as essential for globalised L2 teacher identity, and four means, namely, reflection, sensitivity training on teacher emotion, service learning, and formal training are introduced for nurturing L2 teacher identity for globalisaton.

Wu et al. (in press) encouraged teacher reflection to foster teacher L2 identity for globalisation. He and his colleagues (Wu, et al. in press) advocate transforming the language education curricula to cater to the new needs and to overcome the challenges caused by globalisation. Reflective practices, critical cultural awareness, and reflection on the influences of personal history on their professional attitudes and practices are also offered (Wu 2024, in press) for L2 teachers facing globalisation.

Research

The discoursal approach, suggested in Chapter 3 of this book, can be incorporated into future research in addition to pedagogy on L2 identity. Further research on intercultural competence, global citizenship, and morality, which are under-theorised as mentioned in Chapter 6, can be conducted to increase existing understanding of various aspects of L2 teacher identity. In the same chapter, further research on the relationships of L2 identity with overlapping concepts such as self, self-concept, self-evaluation, self-regulation, metacognition, autonomy, awareness, consciousness, and cognition has been called for.

Novel research methodologies such as the autoethnographic approach which captures real-life, personal narratives, or stories (Borjian 2017), can generate new knowledge of the relationships between language and globalisation, including that on L2 identity (Brock-Utne 2017) from alternative perspectives. Borjian (2017) has compiled an edited volume containing a collection of narratives from linguists, scholars, poets, teachers, and students on how globalisation has influenced their hiatus. Similar novel research methodologies can be devised and adopted to further advance research on how globalisation influences aspects of life that are related to language.

Another area requiring urgent attention is how digitalisation impacts the development of L2 identity. Preliminary discussions and research have been undertaken by researchers such as Chayko (2021), and more attention should be given to this area. This is especially true given the high speed of digital technological progress.

REFERENCES

Akkari, Abdeljalil and Maleq, Katherine. 2020. Rethinking global citizenship education: A critical perspective. In Abdeljalil Akkari and Katherine Maleq (eds.) *Global citizenship education: Critical and international perspectives*, 205–217. Cham: Springer. https://doi.org/10.1007/978-3-030-44617-8_15

Benson, Phil, G. Barkhuizen, Peter Bodycott, and Jill Brown. 2013. *Second language identity in narratives of study abroad.* Houndmills: Palgrave Macmillan. https://doi.org/10.1057/9781137029423.

Block, David. 2014. *Second language identity.* London and New York: Bloomsbury.

Borjian, Maryam. 2017. *Language and globalisation: An autoethnographic approach.* New York and London: Routledge. https://doi.org/10.4324/978 1315394626.

Brock-Utne, Birgit. 2017. Language and identity: Reflections by a cultural commuter. In Maryam Borjian (eds.) *Language and globalisation: An autoethnographic approach,* 132–143. New York and London: Routledge. https://doi.org/10.4324/9781315394626

Chayko, Mary. 2021. The practice of identity: Development, expression, performance, form. In Leah A. Lievrouw and Brian D. Loader (eds.) *Routledge handbook of digital media and communication,* 115–125. London and New York: Routledge. https://doi.org/10.4324/9781315616551

Demuth, Constanze. 2018. Liberalism's all-inclusive promise of freedom and its illiberal effects: A critique of the concept of globalization. In Concha Roldán, Daniel Brauer, and Johannes Rohbeck (eds.) *Philosophy of globalization,* 63–77. Berlin and Boston: Walter de Gruyter. https://doi.org/10.1515/978311 0492415-006

Engel, Laura C., David Rutkowski, and Greg Thompson. 2019. Toward an international measure of global competence? A critical look at the PISA 2018 framework. *Globalisation, Societies and Education* 17 (2): 117–131. https://doi.org/10.1080/14767724.2019.1642183.

Giddens, Anthony. 2006. Modernity and self-identity: Tribulations of the self. In *The discourse reader,* ed. Adam Jaworski and Nikolas Coupland, 415–427. London and New York: Routledge.

Hegel, Georg Wilhelm Friedrich. 1953. *The philosophy of right.* Translated by Thomas Malcolm Knox. Oxford: Oxford University Press.

Hegel, Georg Wilhelm Friedrich. 1977. *Phenomenology of spirit.* Translated by Arnold Vincent Miller. Oxford: Oxford University Press.

Kabir, Russell Sarwar, Brandon Kramer, Mayu Koike, and Aaron C. Sponseller. 2022. Modeling personality antecedents and second language self-efficacy constructs with emerging adults in Japan: Domain-specific matching for assessing global competence in applied contexts. *Frontiers in Psychology* 13: 1032573. https://doi.org/10.3389/fpsyg.2022.1032573.

Kant, Immanuel. 1957. *Perpetual peace.* Englewood Cliffs: Macmillan.

Mallinson, William. 2021. *Guicciardini, geopolitics and geohistory: Understanding inter-state relations.* Cham: Palgrave Macmillan. https://doi.org/10.1007/978-3-030-76537-8_7.

Malovrh, Paul A. 2023. *Second language identity: Awareness, ideology and assessment in higher education*. Cambridge: Cambridge University Press. https://doi.org/10.1017/9781316779798.

Mansilla, Veronica Boix and Wilson, Devon. 2020. What is global competence, and what might it look like in Chinese schools? *Journal of Research in International Education* 19 (1): 3–22. https://doi.org/10.1177/1475240920914089

Matsumoto, Yumi. 2018. Teachers' identities as 'non-native' speakers: Do they matter in English as a lingua franca interactions? In Bedrettin Yazan and Kristen Lindahl (eds.) *Criticality, teacher identity, and (in)equity in English language teaching*, 57–80. https://doi.org/10.1007/978-3-319-72920-6_9

Parmigiani, Davide, Sarah-Louise. Jones, Irma Kunnari, and Elisabetta Nicchia. 2022. Global competence and teacher education programmes. A European Perspective. *Cogent Education* 9 (1): 2022996. https://doi.org/10.1080/2331186X.2021.2022996.

Pashby, Karen, Martha da Costa, Sharon Stein, and Vanessa Andreotti. 2020. A meta-review of typologies of global citizenship education. *Comparative Education* 56 (2): 144–164. https://doi.org/10.1080/03050068.2020.1723352.

Rizvi, Fazal, Bob Lingard, and Rristo Rinne, eds. 2022. *Reimagining globalization and education*. New York: Routledge. https://doi.org/10.4324/9781003207528.

Schenker, Theresa. 2019. Fostering global competence through short term study abroad. *Frontiers: The Interdisciplinary Journal of Study Abroad* XXXI (2): 139–157. https://doi.org/10.36366/frontiers.v31i2.459

Sugiyanto, Devina. 2021. Cultural intelligence of foreign language lecturers: A measurement towards global competence. *Lingua Cultura* 15 (1): 101–108. https://doi.org/10.21512/lc.v15i1.7100

Tarozzi, Massimiliano and Torres, Carlos Alberto. 2016. *Global Citizenship education and the crises of multiculturalism: Comparative perspectives*. London and New York: Bloomsbury. https://doi.org/10.5040/9781474236003

Wu, Manfred Man-fat. 2020. Second language teaching for global citizenship. *Globalisation, Societies and Education* 18 (3): 330–342. https://doi.org/10.1080/14767724.2019.1693349.

Wu, Manfred Man-fat. 2023. *Sublating second language research and practices: Contribution from the Hegelian perspective*. London: Routledge. https://doi.org/10.4324/9781003372240.

Wu, Manfred Man-fat. 2024. Missing links in L2 teaching approaches in the context of globalisation. In *Progress in Education*, vol. 78, ed. Robert V. Nata, 69–94. New York: Nova Science.

Wu, Manfred Man-fat. In press. Harnessing teacher identity for globalisation and internationalisation of TESOL curricula. In Vander Tavares (ed.) *Global and*

critical perspectives on internationalising TESOL teacher education curricula.
    Bristol: Multilingual Matters.
Wu, Manfred Man-fat, Römhild, Ricardo, and Nishizaki, Mona. In press.
    Teaching English as an international language for global citizenship. In Nicola
    Galloway and Ali Fuad Selvi (eds.) *The Routledge handbook of English as an
    international language.* Routledge.
Zajda, Joseph. 2020. *Globalisation, ideology and neo-liberal higher education
    reforms.* Dordrecht: Springer Nature. https://doi.org/10.1007/978-94-024-
    1751-7.

Index

© The Author(s), under exclusive license to Springer Nature Switzerland AG 2024
M. M. Wu, *Globalisation and Second Language Identity*,
https://doi.org/10.1007/978-3-031-68248-3

GPSR Compliance

The European Union's (EU) General Product Safety Regulation (GPSR) is a set of rules that requires consumer products to be safe and our obligations to ensure this.

If you have any concerns about our products, you can contact us on ProductSafety@springernature.com

In case Publisher is established outside the EU, the EU authorized representative is:

Springer Nature Customer Service Center GmbH
Europaplatz 3
69115 Heidelberg, Germany

The manufacturer's authorised representative in the EU is Springer
Nature Customer Service Centre GmbH, Europaplatz 3, 69115 Heidelberg,
Germany. If you have any concerns regarding our products, please
contact ProductSafety@springernature.com

Printed and bound by CPI Group (UK) Ltd, Croydon, CR0 4YY
27/04/2026
02097563-0019